FLORIDA SALTWATER FISHING GUIDE

FLORIDA SALTWATER FISHING GUIDE

MAX BRANYON

TRIBUNE
PUBLISHING

Edited by Dixie Kasper
Designed by Bill Henderson
Cover illustration by Larry Moore
Color illustrations by Jerry Masters
Billfish illustrations and line drawings by Rob Dudley
Back cover photograph by David Cotton
Text photographs courtesy of The Orlando Sentinel, Max Branyon,
Steve Branyon and the Florida Division of Tourism

For information:
Tribune Publishing
P.O. Box 1100, Orlando, Fla. 32802

Printed in the United States

First Edition: May 1988
Second printing: May 1992

Library of Congress Cataloging-in Publication Data

Branyon, Max 1931-
    Florida Saltwater Fishing Guide.
    Includes index.

    1. Fishing–Florida. 2. Marine fishes–Florida.
    3. Fishes–Florida. I. Title.
SH483.B733   1988   799.1'663   88-11364
ISBN 0-941263-04-5

About the Author

Max Branyon writes the fishing forecast for *The Orlando Sentinel*. His column appears daily in the sports section. *Florida Saltwater Fishing Guide* is his fourth book. He is also author of *Florida Freshwater Fishing Guide* and *Florida Boating and Water Sports Guide*, which won first place in the 1985 Florida Outdoor Writers Association competition.

Whether angling for small mangrove snapper or 10-foot marlin, Branyon is in his element when he's saltwater fishing. He's caught them all — sailfish, marlin, wahoo. In 1981, Branyon caught the biggest fish in the 13th Annual Florida Sport Fishing Association Tournament: a 61-pound, 8-ounce wahoo. But he lost a marlin when he dashed into the cabin for a piece of fried chicken and left his rod unattended. The marlin swiped his balao trolling bait.

It was a 20-pound grouper that got him hooked on saltwater fishing when he was 9. Along with his father on a deep-sea fishing trip out of Panama City, Branyon thought he'd hung into a reef as he watched his rod bend double. If the fish had weighed 200 pounds, he couldn't have been prouder, he says now.

"My mother won the jackpot the day before with a 13-pound grouper," Branyon recalls. "Mine was the biggest fish caught aboard the boat that second day, but there was a preacher aboard and the mate was afraid to take up a collection for a jackpot. The $20 would have been nice, but the fish alone was prize enough."

Branyon is a member of Outdoor Writers of America and an executive officer and a member of the board of directors of the Florida Outdoor Writers Association. A former president of the Orange County Sportsmen's Association, he has won awards in fishing, outdoor writing, photography and conservation.

TO MY WIFE, DONNA, AND SONS, STEVE, BOB AND KYLE, AND BROTHER, HUGH

Contents

CHAPTER   PAGES

1 KNOW YOUR FISH 3

2 THE HOT SPOTS 17

3 HOW TO RIG BAITS 35

4 TYING KNOTS 43

5 WHAT, WHERE AND WHEN 51

6 RULES AND REGULATIONS 59

7 SHELLFISH REGULATIONS 63

8 MARINAS 67

9 PIER FISHING 87

10 FISHING TIPS 93

11 FISH FIXIN'S 99

12 CONCLUSION 107

GLOSSARY 109

INDEX 113

FISHERMAN'S DIARY 117

Illustrations

Fish (alphabetically in color)

Barracuda
Striped Bass
Bluefish
Bonefish
Cobia
Dolphin
Drum
Flounder
Grouper
Jewfish
King Mackerel
Spanish Mackerel
Blue Marlin
White Marlin
Mullet
Permit
Pompano
Redfish
Sailfish
Sea Bass
Spotted Sea Trout
Hammerhead Shark
Lemon Shark
Sheepshead
Mangrove Snapper
Mutton Snapper
Red Snapper
Yellowtail Snapper
Snook
Tarpon
Wahoo
Whiting

Lures

Bomber Flair Hair, 12
Boone Striker Trolling Lure, 6
Boone Tout, 11
Diamond Jig, 13
Hawaiian Eye Trolling Lure, 5
Johnny Rattler, 13
Johnson Sprite Spoon, 11
King Getter, 13
Krocodile Lure, 13
Mirrolure, 11
Predator Trolling Rig, 7
Prissy Shad, 13
Rag Mop Trolling Lure, 9
Rapala Shad Rap Lure, 13
Redhead Mirrolure, 10
Red Tail Hawk Jig, 7
Sea Dude, 13
Sea Witch Trolling Lure, 5
Trader Bay Blues Buster, 9
Zara Spook, 13

Hooks, 14-15

Knots, 43-48

Rigs, 35-40

Acknowledgments

Special thanks to the Florida Department of Natural Resources, the Florida Game and Fresh Water Fish Commission, the Florida Division of Tourism, the Division of State Lands, the International Game Fish Association and Central Florida Offshore Anglers. Also, to John Pitts, Ben Beckner, Hank Masson, Tim and T.J. Stallings, Leslie Barnings, Bob Meherg, Jim Chute, Richard Curran, Walt Hudson, Captains Richard Keating, Frank Timmons, Eddie and Derwood Roberts, Phil Lillo, Steve Seaman, Jack Rinehart, Bennie Shipp and Mike Locklear. And to my late fishing pals, Uncle Luther Rowland, Charlie Harris, Lou Houston and Jim Roane.

FLORIDA SALTWATER
FISHING GUIDE

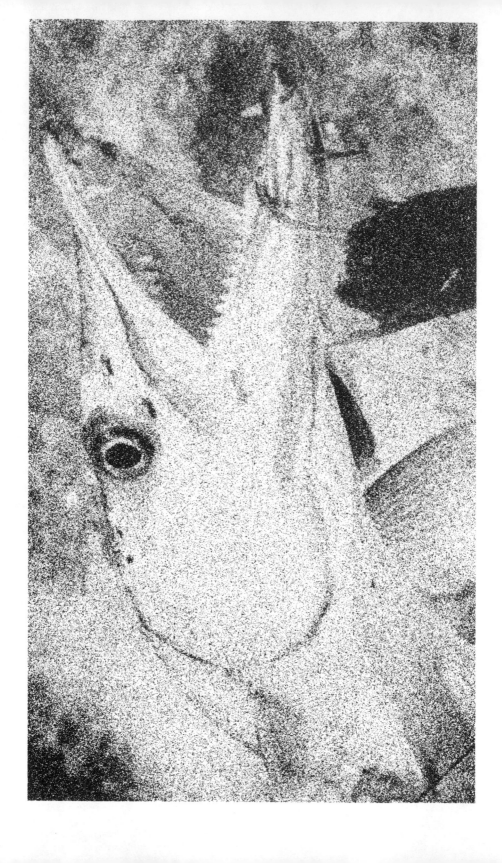

1

Know your fish

When I think about the days I spent fishing as a youngster, my grandmother, who has since passed away, invariably comes to mind. I can still see her in her sun bonnet, sitting in the boat, holding a cane pole, patiently waiting for a fish to bite.

She loved fishing as much as I did. I remember a day when we rowed out in an old wooden skiff we'd borrowed for some saltwater trout fishing. We had never fished that area before, but we had our cane poles and a bucket full of live shrimp. We anchored under a bridge, and it was not long before we were pulling in one silver trout after another.

A sudden storm churned up the water, causing it to slap unmercifully against the bridge pilings. Motorboats passed us as they scooted to shore to avoid the storm. Several boaters offered to take us ashore, but we decided to stay put.

Soon the storm passed. And our dogged determination paid off. We caught trout until we ran out of shrimp.

And I've tried to instill in my sons some of that same sort of excitement as we've shared many an adventure along Florida's coastal and inland waterways: camping on islands, wading the flats for spotted sea trout, trolling for sailfish, marlin, wahoo, king mackerel, and bottom fishing the ocean depths for grouper, snapper, and amberjack, among others.

There's nothing quite like pitching a tent in the shade of an Australian pine on an island along Florida's Intracoastal Waterway. It's the perfect setting for roasting hot dogs over a campfire, telling tales (of the big one that got away, perhaps!), and gazing up at a sky full of stars as you snuggle deeper into a warm sleeping bag. Wading around the island and casting for trout, a brilliant sunrise for a backdrop, is also hard to beat. As the sky comes to life with silent squadrons of pelicans and screaming seagulls, and the water begins to ripple with mullet and baitfish activity, the angler is sure to feel awash with excitement over the prospect of what that day's fishing may bring.

To put it in the words of Chuck McClung, a fishing pal of mine, "You never know what you're going to catch" when it comes to saltwater fishing. How true!

On an early morning trip out of Port Canaveral a few years ago, I was fishing in a boat near Ron Gordon of Orlando. It was Gordon's first trip offshore in the new Fish Nautique he'd bought, and his second offshore trip ever. He had two fishing buddies with him.

Gordon hooked into the largest blue marlin ever caught off Port Canaveral. The big blue weighed more than 420 pounds. We watched as he battled it for 2½ hours before getting it alongside the boat. Russ Fogg and Bobby Houston left our boat and climbed aboard Gordon's to help him boat the marlin. It took all five men to get the fish in the boat. Meanwhile, Lou Houston and I were holding down the other side of the boat to keep it from tipping with five men and a 422-pound marlin.

And then there are the ones that get away. Once, aboard Captains Eddie and Derwood Roberts' Sea Venture out of Port Canaveral, I fished with a man who'd been after sailfish for 10 years without success. The Roberts were seasoned fishermen and the Sea Venture has a great reputation for catching fish. In fact, on my previous trip out on the Sea Venture, a friend, Bill Barnes, had boated a white marlin.

The somewhat down-in-the-mouth angler on this trip explained,

"I've hooked sailfish numerous times during the past 10 years, but they always seem to get off before I can get them to the boat."

Sure enough, during the trip that day, the line popped out of the outrigger and the reel began to scream as a big billfish took the balao (ballyhoo) bait. He grabbed the rod and sat down in the fighting chair. The rest of us figured his luck was about to change.

The fish was a sight as it jumped and leaped. We grabbed our cameras as the fisherman finally wore down the big sail. We cheered as the fish neared the boat. Then, the fish, just above the surface now and just beyond reach, shook his head from side to side and spit out the hook. The fisherman slumped back into the fighting chair.

As we offered him our condolences, he smiled and shook his head. "It may take me another 10 years, but one day I'm going to get a sail."

My sons and I were more fortunate. During our first sailfish trip out of Stuart on Capt. Bennie Shipp's VicKar, we hooked five sailfish at the same time. What pandemonium. We had more sails than we had anglers to man the rods. We each got a sail that day. We released all but one that had been hooked too deeply to live. We had it mounted.

KINDS OF FISH

Sailfish: The sailfish was selected in 1975 by the Florida Legislature as the state's official saltwater fish. The dream of almost every saltwater angler is to catch a sailfish; or if he's caught one, to catch another. They swim so fast and streak through the air in such a blur, that it can be nearly impossible to keep the slack up in the line. My wife, Donna, hooked one of the largest sailfish I've ever seen, but it leaped so many times that we could not jockey the boat around enough to keep the sail from getting slack. It leaped a final time and said goodbye. Fortunately, a 25-pound wahoo caught later that trip was enough to make Donna's day.

Sailfish are often found near the Gulf Stream, but they are also found throughout Florida's coastal waters. Zane Grey, the novelist and outdoorsman, was the first sportsman to introduce sailfishing to Florida around the turn of the century. Before Grey began trolling for sails, king mackerel were the most sought after by offshore anglers.

Most sails weigh less than 55 pounds. However, ones weighing as much as 100 pounds have been caught. Some good trolling baits used to catch sails include Sea Witches and balao combinations, Islander lures, Hawaiian Eyes, Sailures and swimming mullet. Sails will also go after live baitfish.

Sea Witch Trolling Lure

Hawaiian Eye Trolling Lure

The large dorsal fin, looking something like the sail on a ship, blazes a brilliant trail in the sunlight as the sailfish leaps through the air. It is, without a doubt, one of the most exciting fish in the ocean to do battle with. Watching it

rip off line at 60 miles an hour as it does aerial acrobatics is enough to send adrenalin coursing through any angler's veins.

Bureau of Marine Research studies show that the best time to fish for sails is during and after cold fronts. Although it is not known for sure why this is so, speculation is that it is because their feeding activity increases during these times.

Studies by the Florida Department of Natural Resources show that sailfish caught and released can survive. Researchers tagged several sails with sonic tracking devices and followed them for 30 hours, during which time the sailfish showed no signs of irregular behavior.

Many anglers now are measuring sailfish and then releasing them. Taxidermists then can take the measurements and mount a sailfish for your wall with materials they have on hand for creating a realistic trophy. Many angling clubs are also giving certificates to anglers who catch and release sailfish. I have just such a reminder hanging in my den. It reads, "The Stuart Sailfish Club Citation for Outstanding Sport Fishing Accomplishment for catching and releasing a sailfish 84 inches, weight 60 pounds, aboard the charter boat VicKar with Capt. Bennie Shipp."

Blue and white marlin: The blue marlin is the ultimate trophy for an offshore angler. However, considering the number of anglers who ply the offshore reefs and Gulf Stream in search of the heavyweight, very few anglers are fortunate enough to hook, much less boat, a big blue.

Although the blue marlin generally is found in the blue depths in or near the Gulf Stream, the big billfish often cruises in close to shore. Van Mitchell and friends were returning from an offshore trip out of Daytona Beach recently when they spotted something tearing up a school of big dolphin. They didn't even have a line in the water because they were already back to shallower water.

Suddenly they saw a dolphin they guessed to be in the 15-pound range hurled into the air. A huge marlin shot up from underneath and snatched the dolphin in midair. Mitchell quickly grabbed a Penn reel with a C&H Kong artificial lure attached and dropped it in the boat's wake. He no sooner had gotten the lure in the water when a large blue exploded into the air just 20 feet behind the boat's stern with the lure in its mouth. The battle was on! The fisherman was victorious. The whopping 471-pounder was the second largest blue marlin ever caught off the Daytona Beach coast.

A blue marlin usually weighs in at 250 to 300 pounds in Florida waters. However, a white marlin seldom reaches 100 pounds and is more likely to weigh 50 to 60 pounds. Another distinguishing characteristic is that the dorsal fin on the white marlin is spotted and rounded. While the white marlin is not nearly as large as the blue, both are caught with similar baits. C&H lures, Sea Witch and balao combinations, Hawaiian Eyes, whole deboned mullet, Sailfish lures, Barrel Heads, and others are good artificial lures to use for marlin and sailfish. However, many charter captains and other offshore anglers use live bait for marlin and

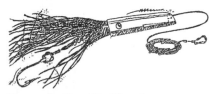

Boone Striker Trolling Lure

sailfish. Blue runners, mullet, pilchards and other live baits are effective billfish lures.

If you hook a marlin or sailfish, you should drop back when the fish hits. In other words, release the reel and let the fish run for several seconds before clicking the reel back into action and setting the hook. Billfish use their bills to attack schools of baitfish with a swordlike action and sometimes hesitate before taking the bait to ensure that it is disabled and ready for the taking. If the drag on the reel is too tight when the hook is set, it will often break the line. A good rule of thumb: Savor the action; don't rush a billfish.

Wahoo: This streamlined fish streaks through the water like a torpedo when hooked and can rip off most of the line on a deep-sea fishing reel on its initial deep-water run. The wahoo is a member of the mackerel family, but unlike the darker meat of the king mackerel, the wahoo's white meat makes it a favorite among seafood lovers. Only sailfish and marlin have given me a battle equal to that of the 61½-pound wahoo I caught in the 1981 Annual Florida Sport Fishing Association Tournament off Port Canaveral. We were using light tackle when the wahoo hit. Before it took my balao-Sea Witch combination, the wahoo took a whole deboned mullet from another angler aboard the boat and attacked the artificial hookless teaser we were trolling behind the boat to attract fish. It stripped most of the hair off the teaser before nailing my lure.

The wahoo is somewhat of a loner. Unlike its cousin, the king mackerel, it doesn't school and is usually found in deep water. However, like the kingfish, the wahoo will go for strip bait when trolled or for deboned mullet and balao.

Predator Trolling Rig

Dolphin: Don't get this saltwater game fish confused with that lovable mammal of television fame, Flipper. The dolphin I'm speaking of is a beautifully colored fish with hues of blue, green and gold. Its fight and taste make it one of the most popular sport fish. Often called the dorado or mahi-mahi, the fish has a head resembling a bulldog's. The males are called bull dolphin and the females, cows. Large numbers of these speedy, scrappy fish often hang around floating lines of sargasso weeds. You can also find them under floating objects, such as boxes, trees, plastic, etc. On a recent trip off New Smyrna Beach, friend Gary Pitts found a floating tree and caught dolphin until his arms nearly fell off.

Once you locate a school of dolphin, keep one on the hook in the water and the other fish in the school will usually hang around. It's fun to watch them light up — their colors get brighter when they're aroused. But that beautiful color soon disappears once the fish are boated and put inside a cooler. For a real colorful show, switch to light spinning tackle and jigs or cut bait and offer that to the schoolies.

Red Tail Hawk Jig

Dolphin will go for live bait, cut bait, squid, trolled balao and skirt combinations and sometimes strip bait. A Sea Witch-balao combination is hard to beat when fishing for dolphin.

Once I was fishing a tournament out of Islamorada in the Florida Keys with my fishing partner, Karl Wickstrom, publisher of *Florida Sportsman* magazine. We had not caught a fish all day. With 35 minutes left in the tournament, I hooked into a barracuda. The sea was so rough that I broke the fighting chair when a wave tossed the boat and slung me into the chair. I sat on the deck while I boated the big barracuda.

Hooking the barracuda was the best thing that happened to us that day. A school of inquisitive dolphin appeared from the deep as I fought the barracuda. Once we got the barracuda into the boat, Karl and I switched to spinning gear and cut bait. We boated more than 50 dolphin in the last half hour of the tournament. We kept a few to eat and released the rest. It was the perfect ending to a rough day.

Barracuda: These toothy predators offer excellent battle when hooked, but be careful when taking them off the hook or you may wind up losing a finger or, worse yet, a hand. Found throughout Florida's coastal waters, the barracuda is more prevalent along the lower regions, especially in the Keys. Once when my sons and I tired of bottom fishing the reefs off Key Largo, we hooked a silver spoon to a trolling rig and wire leader. We had not trolled far before we got into battle with a couple of scrappy barracudas. Bob and Kyle used one for cut bait and filleted and ate the other fish. However, I would not recommend eating barracuda, especially the larger ones caught around the reefs of South Florida. They may have poison in them after feeding on smaller fish that have fed on poisonous coral.

Anglers who have trolled Florida's offshore waters surely have known barracuda to cut off balao, mullet and strip bait. Most anglers probably also know the frustration of reeling in a fish that became dinner for a barracuda on its way to the boat. Although the silvery fish sometimes exceeds 100 pounds, most are much smaller with many weighing 10 pounds or less.

Amberjack: Anyone who has ever fought a big amberjack knows what a tiring experience it can be. These game fighters like to hang around offshore wrecks and reefs and will readily take a live baitfish offered them.

A fishing buddy, Marion Coffey, fought two in the 60- to 70-pound class back to back one day. A husky football coach, Coffey was ready for the bench after battling the second one to the boat. On another trip, my brother Bill, his wife Betty, and I were fishing aboard Capt. Frank Timmons party boat, the Marianne, when we hit a school of big amberjacks. The scene can only be described as one of mass hysteria. People were screaming, lines were breaking or crossing and getting tangled. But the captain stayed in the same spot until everyone aboard had caught at least one amberjack.

Fishing out of Port Canaveral on one of Frank Brawley's head boats, I saw an angler on my left fighting a big amberjack to the boat's stern. Meanwhile, the fisherman to my right was baiting his hook. My bait was on the bottom.

"If you'll drop your bait over here there's a big amberjack following the one that's hooked," I said. "I believe you can hook it."

He dropped his bait over the side near the big amberjack that weighed at least 50 pounds. However, the drag on his reel was set too tightly and when the jack hit, it yanked the fisherman overboard and snapped his rod in half. I grabbed the angler by the left pocket of his jeans and the fisherman to his right grabbed his other pocket. We managed to pull him back aboard, but not until he'd held on to the rod and reel for a bit before deciding to let it and the big fish go.

Fishing out of Islamorada aboard the Captain Jack fishing boat, I hooked a large amberjack, and after fighting it up from several hundred feet of water, all I reeled in was the head. The hammerhead shark that had devoured the rest of the fish was circling below the boat. The mate and I put together a rig with a chain leader and hooked the amberjack head through the eyes and offered the rest of the fish to the big shark.

After circling several times, the shark took the head and the fight was on. We battled the big shark for more than an hour before bringing it alongside the boat.

Sharks: Although sharks usually swim unhurriedly throughout Florida's waterways, they have been clocked at almost 30 miles per hour going after trolled bait. Makos and other sharks can offer a battle akin to any gamefish, including marlin and sailfish. Many of the several hundred species in Florida's waters are edible and even considered a delicacy by some. If you go fishing for sharks, nighttime is the best time to fish for these nocturnal creatures.

It's best to exercise some caution with sharks — particularly once you've boated them. Once, fishing aboard the Sea Venture out of Port

Canaveral, I caught a 100-pound lemon shark around an old Dutch wreck about 10 miles out. The shark had been lying on the deck — gutless and bloodless — for a good 30 minutes when I decided to take a better look. When I was a couple of feet away from the shark, it leaped into the air and its jaws slammed into the stern of the boat where it clung doggedly for at least five minutes before releasing its grip and dropping back down to the deck. Six years later, on another trip aboard the Sea Venture, I noticed the teeth marks were still there.

When it comes to sharks, there's surely no lack of excitement.

A favorite shark-fishing site of my son's is the Ten Thousand Islands area of the Everglades. When the mosquitoes and sand gnats aren't too fierce at night, Kyle likes to fish the inside holes around the oyster bars near Chokoloskee. He uses whole dead fish and chunks of bloody cut bait. On one trip he caught a big shark on a whole fish. He rebaited with another whole fish. Line began to peel off the reel. When he set the hook, he was more than a little surprised to see a giant tarpon leap from the water.

On a deep-sea fishing trip out of Port Canaveral, my son Steve decided it would be nice to take a swim with one of his buddies when offshore trolling got to be a little slow. I advised against it. The blood from a blackfin tuna we'd just caught was trailing beind the boat. It wasn't long before we spotted a big fin following the boat. A large hammerhead had picked up the trail. There was no more talk of swimming that day.

It is wise not to bring a shark aboard a small boat. Even when handling a shark aboard a large boat, care must be taken not to ag-

gravate the fish. Some of the more docile sharks — basking, whale and even the peaceful nurse — can be goaded into being a menace on occasion.

Among the sharks most feared are the hammerhead, mako, tiger, brown and the great white, which has been spotted in Florida's offshore waters. There are about 350 species of sharks that frequent area waters. Many of them, including small puppy sharks, offer a good fight and some tasty eating.

Bluefish: Blues, as they're often called, are scrappy gamefish predators that roam Florida's coastal waters in schools and can often be found in a feeding frenzy ripping into schools of baitfish. They are great fighters and fairly tasty if they're bled immediately after they're caught. To do this, slit their throats, pack them in ice and soak them in milk or brine for several hours before cooking.

Trader Bay Blues Buster

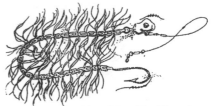
Rag Mop Trolling Lure

When blues are feeding, they will hit spoons, plugs such as a strange looking Ragmop that is a good trolling bait, and live bait such as shrimp and finger mullet. However, one of their favorite baits is fresh mullet cut into chunks and fished on the bottom. Bluefish average from one to three pounds, but many in the five- to 15-pound class are caught in Florida waters, especially during the cooler months of the year.

Bonefish: Found mostly in the Florida Keys, this gray ghost of Florida's coastal waters can rip off 100 yards of line before you can bat an eye. Guides ply the Keys on both sides in search of these skittish fish. They pole along the flats and sight fish for the wily bonefish, which can sometimes be spotted feeding and stirring up the bottom in search of small crustaceans. Anglers must cast their shrimp, artificial fly or other lures used for bonefish just right so as not to spook the fish and send it scurrying to deeper water. The bonefish is one of the most difficult fish to catch in Florida. It's wise to hire a guide — at least the first time out. Bonefish vary from three to 10 pounds; however, they can weigh as much as 20 pounds. Because they're not good eating, it's best to take a picture and release the fish to do battle another day.

Permit: Most Florida anglers will never see a permit unless they are fishing with a guide or a veteran angler. The permit is usually much larger and more easily spooked than the bonefish. While most are caught by poling the flats along the shallows of the Keys, they are found in other Florida waters as well. Capt. Richard Keating, a Marathon fishing guide, uses light fishing line and poles the shallow flats of the Gulf and Atlantic throughout the Keys in search of the permit, his favorite fish. "When you hook a 25-pound permit on light tackle, you're in for an hour-and-a-half to two-hour battle," Keating said.

"The permit feels very vulnerable in real shallow water anyway," said Keating, "and if you toss your bait too close to him and spook him, he's gone to deeper water pronto." The permit usually averages from 10 to 20 pounds but can reach 50 pounds. Small live or dead crabs are good bait for permit. So are small jigs and sometimes flies. While permit are good eating, most sportsmen release these sporting fish.

Tarpon: These silver kings offer some of the best battle around. While they can be found year-round in the Ten Thousand Islands and the Florida Keys, anglers will find them throughout Florida's waters as they migrate up and down the coast. These aerial acrobats have been known to jump into boats when hooked. If this happens, get as far away from the fish as possible because they can tear up a boat with their powerful bodies. Never try to boat a "green" tarpon, one that has not been fought until it is tired. You could be in for big trouble if you do. The tarpon is a large fish — some of the ones caught in Florida have weighed as much as 200 pounds.

Tarpon will hit many types of baits and lures: flies, live pinfish, cut bait, whole dead or live mullet, and many types of lures. The first two tarpon I hooked hit a Mirrolure that I was casting along a channel while wading the flats near Merritt Island. I was using ultra-light tackle with 4-pound test line.

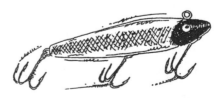

Redhead Mirrolure

And although neither fish stayed on for more than one jump each, it was a thrilling experience.

Tarpon make for some poor eating, so release them when you catch them. Their mouths are extremely tough and the angler must really set the hook if he expects to hang on to them. Even then, you'll lose more than you catch, but the battle is fun. June of '91 was a memorable time for me — I battled 10 tarpon in one day at Boca Grande.

Pompano: These scrappy little fish are a gourmet's delight. They can be prepared many different ways. Its streamlined body resembles that of a permit, but the pompano is much smaller. Found throughout Florida's coastal waters, a pompano hits best in the surf on sand fleas (sand crabs). It also will hit live shrimp and small jigs on light tackle. The common Florida pompano, which usually weighs between one and five pounds, can be found along shallow sand flats, inlets and piers. Other types of pompano found in Florida waters are round and African pompano. Neither can match the common pompano in taste, however. While the common and round species are caught along the shallow inshore waters, the much larger African pompano is found along the deep offshore reefs.

Redfish: Also known as the channel bass, this popular Florida fish became endangered quickly when the Cajun-style redfish dish became popular and netters began going for even the big reds that were considered poor eating before the spicy recipe became a hit. Because of their scarcity, a limit of one fish has been imposed and the fish are off-limits in March, April and May.

Reds are strong, dogged fighters. The first red I caught while wading the Indian River fought me for more than an hour before I beached it at the opposite end of the island from where I had hooked the 18½-pounder. Using light tackle and a Mirrolure plug, I enjoyed the action immensely. Often I would get the redfish near me until it spotted me and then it would head for deeper water, taking most of my line with it.

Boone Tout

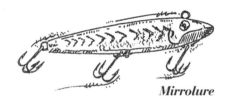

Mirrolure

Johnson Sprite Spoon

Reds migrate throughout Florida's coastal waters, feeding on small crustaceans. Look for them in the surf, the bays, intracoastal waterways and inlets. You can find them year-round in the Chokoloskee-Everglades City area and in the Florida Keys. Reds are a bronze color and have a single black spot on their tails. However, I have, on occasion, caught redfish with numerous spots on their lower body. Artificial lures such as Sea Dudes, Trout Touts and other grubs, spoons and other lures are good for catching redfish. So are live shrimp, small crabs, fingerling mullet and pinfish. Redfish are fair eating, but it is best to release them because of their scarcity.

Snook: This is one of the most sought-after fish in Florida. Hooking into a 20-pound snook is akin to snagging a 20-pound bass. When hooked, the snook may leap through the air many times and head for the nearest mangrove or oyster bar. Anglers get hooked so on snook that they spend much of their spare time searching for them.

One of the best snook fisherman I had the pleasure of knowing was the late Jim Roane of Winter Park, who was known as the dean of snook fishermen. I was with Jim when he caught a 25-pound snook at low tide deep in the Everglades. When he died at 84, Jack Myers, his son, Mark, and I did as he'd requested and scattered his ashes among his favorite fishing holes around the mangrove islands of the Ten Thousand Islands area near Chokoloskee.

When my son, Bob, was about 5, we were snook fishing with Bob Lundquest and his son, Ricky, near Gordon's Pass at Naples. We were trolling near the thick mangrove country with heavy-duty rods, reels and lines and big artificial lures for big snook. My son reached for a lightweight casting rod with a Mirrolure tied to the end of a light monofilament line. He didn't want to use the big rod and reel. I indulged him and let him drop the lure in the boat's wake. Soon there was quite a commotion as a big snook inhaled the lure and backlashed the line in the process. And as if this weren't enough, Lundquest, who was operating the outboard motor, hooked a snook, which proceeded to leap into the air

and leave the plug hanging in a mangrove limb about four feet above the water's surface. All this while we were trying to buck a strong tide in a narrow channel.

My son finally boated his snook — it weighed 15 pounds and was nearly as long as my son was tall — and we retrieved Lundquest's plug from the tree.

Snook fishing does have its share of exciting moments. Dressed in a long lateral black stripe it uses for a sonar device, the snook is unpredictable when hooked and can offer the fishing thrill of a lifetime.

Snook are found mostly in the lower half of Florida's waters in both the Atlantic and Gulf of Mexico. They can be found around inlets, in the surf, around bridges, warm water at power plants during cold weather and around oyster bars and rocks. They feed during the day, but are very active at night. They will hit live shrimp, many different types of artificial lures, including Snook Slayers, Mirrolures, Bombers, bucktail jigs, grubs, Zara Spooks and spoons. They also will hit live pinfish, finger mullet, shrimp and ladyfish fished on the bottom. When it comes to dinner, snook is the filet mignon of fish.

Bomber Flair Hair

Highly acclaimed for their fighting ability, excellent flavor and accessibility, snook do have some reprieve from anglers: Closed seasons are January, February, June, July and August. Snook caught during these months must be released. Additionally, there is a minimum size requirement of 24 inches. An angler can have only two snook in his or her possession and only one can be over 34 inches.

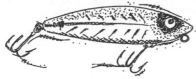

Zara Spook

Best of the rest: Other popular fish include the sea trout, snapper, grouper, flounder, sheepshead, cobia, king mackerel, Spanish mackerel, whiting, tripletail, striped bass and drum.

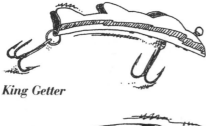

King Getter

Diamond Jig

Krocodile Lure

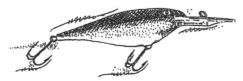

Rapala Shad Rap Lure

One of my favorites is the sea trout, or spotted sea trout. I enjoy catching them on spoons, Sea Dudes, Johnny Rattler surface

lures, jigs, grubs and other artificials. Sea trout are caught in large numbers in the fall and winter. They spend virtually their entire lives in estuaries, moving only occasionally to the mouth of the estuaries and coastal waters.

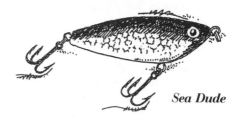

Sea Dude

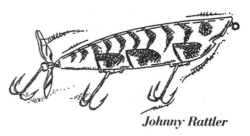

Johnny Rattler

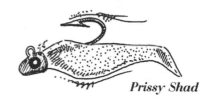

Prissy Shad

Snapper and grouper are taken primarily in offshore waters. Charter boats, head boats (boats that charge by the head) and pleasure boats ply the offshore reefs and ledges where these species live. Most snapper and grouper tend to live long and grow slow. A life span of 20 years or more is not uncommon. Red snapper may weigh in at 30 to 35 pounds, but catches generally average five to 10 pounds.

Seven species of grouper — gag, black, Nassau, red, yellowfin, yellowmouth and scamp — are protected by a 20-inch minimum size limit. Red and gag grouper are the most frequently caught grouper in the Gulf of Mexico; Nassau and black grouper are more commonly caught on the east coast and in the Keys. Jewfish are now protected and must be released. Cut bait, squid, live baitfish, whole sardines and other baits are good bets for grouper and snapper. Grouper may range from a few pounds to several hundred pounds.

Flounder, a flat fish that lies on the bottom and buries in the sand to wait for its prey, is one of the most tasty of the saltwater species. Ironically, it is born with eyes on both sides of its head, but one eye moves to the other side at an early stage of development so that both eyes are situated side by side, which makes it easier for the fish to spot any baitfish that happen by. Fishing on a sandy bottom with live shrimp or live fingerling mullet is an effective way to catch flounder. However, their bite is so slight that it takes an alert angler to catch them.

KINDS OF HOOKS

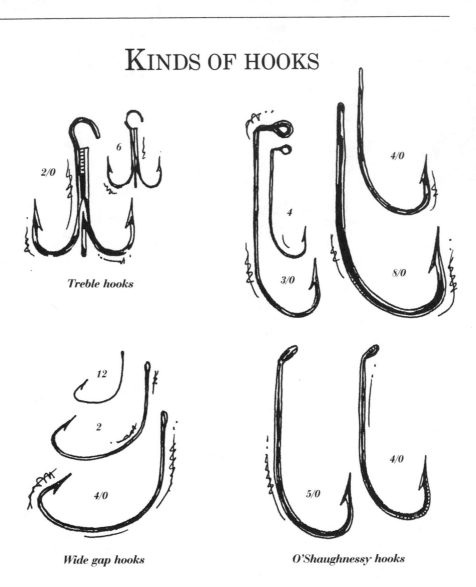

Treble hooks

Wide gap hooks

O'Shaughnessy hooks

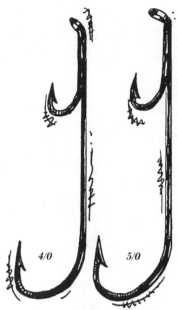

Ryder hooks

4/0   5/0

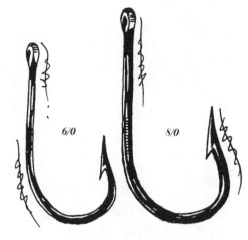

6/0   8/0

Tarpon and tuna hooks

6   7

Flounder hooks

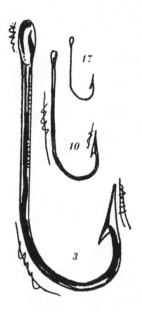

17

10

3

Kirby sea hooks

Beak hooks

2

THE HOT SPOTS

BY WAY OF INTRODUCTION

Fish are affected by the water temperatures and other factors. This chapter, dealing with some of Florida's hottest spots during each month of the year, will help you decide where to fish for the fish you want to catch.

With help from the Florida Department of Natural Resources, I have listed coordinates to help you find these hot spots. So, whether you plan to fish in comfort in spring, fall and sometimes winter, or whether you prefer the heat of the summer, this chapter will give you an overview of where to fish those months.

Florida has 8,000 miles of coastline, barrier islands, estuaries, keys and mangrove islands. The state Department of Natural Resources has done extensive studies on how changing seasons affect the migration of Florida's saltwater fish. For example, Spanish and king mackerel migrate northward along both coasts. During the winter, they are plentiful in the ocean off the middle and south keys, from Fort Pierce to Boynton Beach on the Atlantic and off Naples and Fort Myers in the Gulf.

Anglers would do well to acquaint themselves with migration patterns.

JANUARY

Most fishing offshore along the upper east coast is done 16 to 22 miles out. A good site for grouper and snapper is 20 miles offshore between St. Augustine and Daytona Beach. This area has 3 square miles of hard sand and shell bottom at the 108-foot depth. To find it, take this course: 29°36'N 80°23'W.

For inshore angling, try the inlets for sea trout, redfish, drum and flounder. Sheepshead hit best around the jetties. Bluefish are around the piers and in the inlets. For whiting and pompano, fish in the surf with sand fleas, shrimp or clams. If you like American shad fishing, try the St. Johns River east of Sanford. Rental boats are available at Lemon Bluff Fish Camp, Osteen Bridge Fish Camp and other sites on state roads 520 and 50. The area from Mullet Lake Park to Lemon Bluff is one of the hottest spots on the river. Troll shad rigs for best results. Shad have tender mouths, so don't rush them once you've hooked them. Anglers sometimes release shad that migrate inward from the ocean to spawn. Shad roe is considered a delicacy by others. Although they are a bit on the bony side, other fishermen like to bake shad for hours in the oven for some tasty eating.

Sailfish angling is usually hitting its peak in January along the lower east coast. Other gamefish hitting in the Gulf Stream during this time include marlin, dolphin, bonito, wahoo, tuna, amberjack, barracuda and both Spanish and king mackerel.

Head boats — boats that charge by the person, or head, and are also called party boats — usually catch bottom fish while drifting the southeast coast. Grouper and snapper are tops on the preferred dining list. However, sea bass, triggerfish and grunts offer decent eating as well.

Halfway between Palm Beach and Fort Lauderdale along the outer reefs, North East Hole is a good site for bottom fish. This 120-foot water has structures of scattered rock and coral growth. Set your course for 26°20'N 80°03'W.

Surf fishing is best for croaker, whiting, pompano, bluefish, sea trout and Spanish mackerel. Sea trout are best in the upper Keys to Cape Sable, while redfish, or red drum, can be found more often in Florida Bay. Mangrove snapper and bonefish can be found throughout the area.

Offshore trolling is good for sails, Spanish and king mackerel. Offshore bottom fishing is good, too, especially along the lower gulf coast between Fort Myers Beach and Naples, about 8 miles offshore. For red and black grouper and grunts, try using cut and live bait to fish the sand and shell bottom holes and rock ledges from 40 to 60 feet deep. Course: 26°17'N 82°17'W.

To the north on the gulf is another good fishing spot, about 15 miles west of St. Petersburg in 120- to 130-foot water. This mud and sand bottom with patches of rocks offers some good catches of grouper and red snapper during the winter.

Fish the passes and deep-water channels for redfish and trout. If you're looking for sheepshead, fish with live shrimp or fiddler crabs around Manatee County's bridges and pilings.

Sheepshead and trout usually frequent the rivers and creeks of the northwest coast. Redfish are plentiful in Spring Creek at Oyster Bay, 27 miles south of Tallahassee, and at the mouths of other rivers and passes in the Panhandle.

On decent January days, party boats head for the offshore reefs for snapper and grouper. Some of the best red snapper fishing this time of year can be found between

Panama City and Pensacola.

Snook can be found in the estuaries of the Atlantic north of Vero Beach and at Sebastian Inlet. The linesiders are also present at Chokoloskee and the Ten Thousand Islands area of the gulf and at Tampa Bay and other sites. Don't forget, though, they must be released in January, February, June, July and August.

FEBRUARY

Striped bass move into the St. Johns and St. Marys rivers for some good inside action. Inshore angling for sea trout, redfish and sheepshead is usually good along the upper east coast, mostly in creeks, rivers and along the Intracoastal Waterway. Bluefish angling is more productive from the piers.

When it comes to weather, February can be a bear of a month. But all is not lost. Red snapper and grouper fishing is popular this time of year. A good site for both is an exposed reef with a rolling, hard sand bottom about 20 miles offshore between Mayport and St. Augustine in 18 to 22 fathoms (a fathom is 6 feet) Course: 23°58' to 30°10'N 80°33'W.

Along the lower east coast, offshore trolling is excellent in the Gulf Stream for sailfish, marlin, king mackerel and wahoo. For amberjack and barracuda, one of the best spots is Amberjack Hole, which is the boom of a crane found between Fort Lauderdale and Miami just inshore of the third reef in 65- to 76-foot water (25°52'N 80°05'W).

Bluefish, pompano and Spanish mackerel can be caught in the Intracoastal Waterway. And while they are not present in great number, tarpon can sometimes be found around creeks and inlets in the southeastern area. For cobia, fish the piers and inlet jetties.

For the best tarpon fishing during February, try fishing around bridges and canals in the Florida Keys. The best trout and redfish angling can be found in Florida Bay.

Because the Keys are a hot spot for winter fishing, anglers should make arrangements for boats and lodging well in advance.

One of the best fishing spots for king and cero mackerel is a large area of grass, shell and rock bottom in 54- to 120-foot water southeast of the Dry Tortugas known as No Man's Land. (24°40' to 25° 00'N 81°55' to 82°43'W.)

Trout and snook fishing is good along the lower Gulf, especially in the creeks and canals. For redfish, fish the oyster bars and bridges. Mangrove snapper hit best in the creeks and over the bars.

From Bradenton to Cape San Blas on the upper gulf coast, the fishing is good for sheepshead around the pilings and bridges and sea trout and redfish in the deepwater channels and in rivers and creeks.

For black grouper and grunts, a good hole is situated some 15 miles west of Tarpon Springs in 50 to 70 feet of water. The bottom is made up of sand and shell with rock areas as high as 14 feet. (28°08'N 83°13'W.)

If it's inshore fishing you're out for, try along the northwest gulf coast in the surf for whiting; in the bayous and river mouths for reds, and in the rivers and bays for sea trout.

Offshore fishing is excellent out of Destin for red, vermillion and porgy snapper, and gag grouper.

Fish 25 miles south of Destin along a large shell area that has ridges and rock cliffs. The water is 198 to 246 feet deep at this site. (29°51'N 86°30'W).

Remember: You can't keep snook in February. And check redfish regulations to see if there have been any changes.

MARCH

This is the best month to catch the popular American shad in the St. Johns River from Lemon Bluff to Puzzle Lake. Troll small shad rigs, a combination of small jigs and spoons. Once you've found the right depth and trolling speed, you usually can come up with some scrappy saltwater shad. Another way is to find a school of shad to cast into. Either way, be sure to stash a landing net in your boat. Because of their tender mouths, shad often are lost before anglers can get them in the boat.

Offshore fishing along the northeast coast is good for yelloweye (silk), red and vermillion snapper that congregate in a 2-mile square-shaped area 25 miles offshore between Daytona Beach and St. Augustine in water that's as deep as 900 feet with a 360-foot peak. (20°44'N 80°13'W).

Bluefish, king mackerel, cobia, marlin, sailfish, bonito, wahoo and barracuda can be caught by trolling the Gulf Stream along the lower east coast. Blue marlin have been known to feed on large bluefish that migrate in schools down the eastern coast to Florida each year.

The Florida Keys offer some of the best inshore fishing for trout, snook and redfish. Try fishing around the bridges of Florida Bay. Bonefish hit well along the flats on both the Gulf and Atlantic sides. Sailfish, king and Spanish mackerel hit best offshore. Also, good grouper and snapper fishing can be found along all the reefs in this area. An excellent location is R.W. Flats, which is south of the Dry Tortugas in 32 to 36 fathoms and consists of coral rock and three sunken submarines. (24°45' to 25°00'N 83°40'W).

Along the lower gulf coast, try fishing the flats and canals for sea trout. For snook, try the rivers and canals and for mangrove snapper and redfish, fish the creeks and oyster bars. Sheepshead can best be found around the bridges and pilings.

For red and gag grouper and grunt, try "245 Degrees from Longboat Pass," a 408- to 444-foot deep sandy area with large rock formations. (20°51'N 82°56'W).

Snook fishing is excellent in Manatee County around the canals and basins. Trout and redfish can be found in the passes and deep-water channels. Sheepshead hit best around the bridges, especially around the Sunshine Skyway Bridge between Palmetto and St. Petersburg.

March is a good month for grouper, red snapper and grunt fishing in an area 10 miles west of Clearwater in 80- to 100-foot water. Here, the sloped bottom is covered with coral, sponge, rock and shell. (27°58'N 83°28'W).

This is also the month that cobia start their migration along the northwest gulf coast and can be caught from piers, boats and in the surf. They travel in pods of four or more fish and will hit almost anything you toss to them: lure or live bait. Trout and reds are still in the bayous, river mouths and lagoons.

Offshore head boats usually fish around the 240-foot curve during March for grouper, scamp and red snapper. The curve is a reef off Dunedin, due west of Hurricane Pass some 80 nautical miles. The bottom varies from 21 to 36 fathoms.

APRIL

Head boats start running daily trips instead of just weekend outings from the ports along the northeast coast to the offshore reefs for red snapper and grouper. A good Central Florida spot for both is located 25 miles off New Smyrna Beach in water that ranges in depth from 138 to 204 feet.

Inshore fishing is good for trout in the Matanzas River and along the grass flats. For bluefish and whiting, try the inlets and the surf. For flounder, try the bays. Bluefish, whiting and pompano show up in the surf and around the ocean piers along the lower east coast. Snook hit best in the canals and inlets, while trout can be found along the Indian River grass flats.

For anglers plying the offshore reefs in trolling boats, fishing is good for sailfish, dolphin and king mackerel. And for those who prefer bottom fishing from head boats and drift boats, grouper and snapper offer some good fishing. A good location for both trolling and bottom fishing is off Atlantic Boulevard just north of Fort Lauderdale in 100 to 150 feet of water. It is off the third reef and has a ragged bottom of heavy coral growth (26°14'N 80°03'W).

The Keys offer some offshore fishing for sailfish, but inshore fishing is more popular in April for most anglers. In the upper Keys, back country and Florida Bay, the most popular fish are snook, sea trout and redfish. For bonefish, fish the flats along these areas. For tarpon, try the bridges and channels.

As the water warms during April, fishing improves along the lower gulf coast. Trout and redfish stay inside the bays and canals until hot weather sets in and forces them to deeper water. Sheepshead and mangrove snapper are found in Charlotte Harbor around the docks and bridges. Whiting and silver trout are found most frequently in the surf and canals.

Offshore trolling is good for king and Spanish mackerel along the southwest coast. Head boats go in search of grouper along the ocean bottom. An excellent location for grouper, cobia, king and Spanish mackerel is the Ice Box, an area 5 miles southeast of Sarasota in 50-foot water. The bottom is heavy rock with numerous gullies. (27°10' to 27°16'N 82°47'W).

Along the northwest gulf coast, head boats begin daily runs in search of red snapper, the fish of choice in this area. Also, king and Spanish mackerel begin showing up and grouper fishing improves throughout the area. A good grouper spot is located 10 miles south of Carrabelle where the bottom is sand with rock and shell ridges. (29°33' to 29°48'N 84°35'W).

The cobia run is at its peak in April. Trolling boats are kept busy in their search for Spanish mackerel, bonito, dolphin and cobia. Sailfishing picks up later in the month.

Inshore fishing in the surf and from piers is good for whiting, cobia, spadefish, bluefish and pompano. Bluefish can be found in the bays; trout frequent grass flats, lagoons and bays; sheepshead hang around pilings.

MAY

Along the upper east coast, red and vermillion snapper and grouper hit well along the offshore reefs. A good location is the East Grounds, 25 miles east of Mayport in 27 to 28 fathoms. (30°22'N 80°54'W). It has a rolling, hard sand bottom, and rocks and coral. Offshore trolling boats also will find king mackerel taking the bait.

Inshore, the grass flats are good sites for sea trout. Try the Matanzas, Indian and Banana rivers for best results. Redfish can be found in inlets and around Mosquito Lagoon near Titusville and Oak Hill. Drum and sheepshead hit around the bridges and pilings. Bluefish and whiting are best found in the surf and around ocean piers.

Surf fishing is good and so are the inlets along the lower east coast for blues, whiting, pompano, snook, African pompano and jack crevalle. These also can be caught from piers. Trout and snook are in the Indian River and in the inlets and canals.

Offshore fishing is good for sailfish, king mackerel, dolphin and little tunny. Bottom fishing is best done from drift boats, which may snag sailfish, kings, dolphin and bonito.

A good site for red and vermillion snapper, red grouper, grunts and triggerfish is the 73-foot Ridge, 15 miles east of Melbourne in 72- to 84-foot water. This reef of coral rock is a good spot for assorted bottom fish. (28°13'N 80°12' to 80°15'W).

And in the Keys, May is a hot month for tarpon. Fish the passes and under the bridges throughout the area for these line-busting "silver kings." The upper Keys are good for redfish and snook, while bonefish can be caught here and in the middle Keys. Sailfish are a good bet offshore and some anglers go for swordfish along the east coast. However, there has been a decline in swordfish in recent years.

Southeast of Key West is an excellent spot for assorted snapper and grouper. Try fishing a rock cliff in 9 to 20 fathoms. (24°25'N 82°03'W).

If you're looking for jewfish, grouper and cobia along the lower gulf coast, try three miles offshore between Naples and Fort Myers

Beach. Mud Hole is a freshwater spring with steep rocky sides in 60-foot water. Look for a boil of discolored water. (about 26°11'N 82°01'W).

For trout and redfish, try fishing the bays and creeks where both species congregate. For snook, fish the passes. Snapper and sheepshead can be found around bridges and docks. Whiting are plentiful in the surf. For king and Spanish mackerel, go offshore.

Trout fishing improves along the upper gulf coast. They frequent the flats as water warms. Redfish can be found around inshore rocks. You'll find tarpon mostly in the rivers and inshore around oyster bars.

Trolling boats go for Spanish mackerel all along the upper gulf coast. Grouper fishing is good over the offshore rock piles.

A fruitful site for some offshore bottom fishing is about 25 miles southeast of Steinhatchee in 30- to 54-foot water. It has a flat bottom with rock ridges. (28°47' to 20°04'N 83°26' to 83°29'W).

Cobia continue their migration along the northwest gulf coast. Spanish and king mackerel migrations follow.

Inshore fishing for trout is best along the grass flats. Surf fishing is good for whiting, blues and pompano. Some tarpon can be caught in the bays.

Destin and Panama City are hot spots for red snapper, grouper, warsaw and scamp. A good area can be found 20 miles offshore between the two cities in 17 to 23 fathoms in a spot called 3-5s. It has a sand bottom with sharp ledges 3 to 5 fathoms in relief. (29°46' to 30°04'N 85°50' to 86°23'W).

JUNE

This is the peak month for saltwater fishing in Florida. Along the upper east coast, fishing is good for amberjack, sailfish and grouper. An excellent area for Spanish and king mackerel and bonito is the sea buoy off Mayport. The bottom is hard sand with patches of shell and grass and some scattered, low rocks 42 to 60 feet deep. (30°27'N 81°18'W).

You'll find sea trout in the rivers and along the grass flats. In the surf, around the inlets and piers, look for whiting and pompano. Fish the rivers and bays for flounder and drum.

Trout are also in the Indian River along the lower east coast, especially along the shallow grass flats and sand bars. For croaker, bluefish, pompano and whiting, fish in the surf.

Offshore, king mackerel and sailfish are in the Gulf Stream and dolphin can be found along the weed lines — you'll discover that's where most of the trolling boats go in search of these gamefish. Bottom fishing and drift fishing boats can find grouper, snapper and little tunny. Also, drift boats sometimes luck into king mackerel and sailfish while drifting the offshore reefs.

In the Keys, trout and redfish frequent the upper Keys. Tarpon and mangrove snapper are at home throughout the Keys. For the wily bonefish, you're liable to have better results fishing the shallow flats of the upper and middle Keys on both the Atlantic and Gulf sides. Most trolling boats go for sailfish during June. For the tasty yellowtails, try fishing the conch reefs offshore between Islamorada and Marathon. Mutton, mangrove snapper and grouper hit well on these reefs also. You'll find the reefs, with their patches of high coral, in 25- to 65-foot water. (24°57'N 80°27'W).

Tarpon are active along the lower gulf coast along the beaches and in the bays. June is the month when hundreds of tarpon are hooked and released in tournament fishing.

Offshore, Spanish and king mackerel can be caught by trolling boats when the wind is not too strong.

Grouper is the favorite among bottom fishermen in June. A good site is about 20 miles off Bradenton in 90- to 120-foot water where the bottom is made up of sand and shell with some rock, sponge and coral.

Inshore, trout and shellfish can be found inside the bays and creeks. For sheepshead and mangrove snapper, fish in the sounds around bridges and docks. For whiting and silver trout (weakfish), fish around the piers, bridges, in the canals and in the surf.

Around the upper gulf coast, trout will have moved into the grass flats. Try the rivers for sheepshead, and river mouths and oyster bars in those areas for tarpon. For redfish, try fishing the inshore oyster bars and rock piles. Offshore fishing is best for Spanish mackerel.

For cobia, fish any offshore buoy or other marker. The best way to catch them is to anchor uptide from the marker and cast jigs toward the buoy. Another effective method is to drift live bait such as fingerling mullet toward the buoy. Other cobia usually will follow a hooked one to the boat, so keep an extra rod rigged nearby.

Snook fishing is closed.

JULY

Good fishing continues — especially along the upper east coast — for dolphin, amberjack, sailfish and king mackerel. Along the Central Florida Atlantic coast, red and black grouper hit in an area called Half North and East 11 Grounds, which is about 15 miles off New Smyrna Beach. The bottom is a ridge of coral cliffs about two miles long and is surrounded by sand and shell, 66 to 78 feet deep. (29°02' to 29°05'N 80°29' to 80°33'W).

Inshore fishing is good for trout along the grass flats at Mosquito Lagoon and the Intracoastal Waterway. Fish around bridges for drum. For redfish, try fishing the surf and inlets, but release them when they are not in season. Regulations change from time to time to protect this endangered fish.

Lower east coast fishing is good around piers and bridges for tarpon, jack crevalle and ladyfish. All three put up a good fight. Biscayne Bay is good for mangrove snapper, small grouper, bonefish, permit and trout.

Offshore angling is good for sailfish, bonito, dolphin, white and blue marlin, tuna, shark, wahoo and king mackerel, especially in the Gulf Stream and along the outer reefs. Bottom fishing and drift fishing is best for snapper, grouper and assorted others.

Coffin's Patch is a good spot for sailfish, dolphin, bonito, barracuda, king mackerel and others. Coffin's Patch is the edge of the main reef in an area of scattered shipwrecks and heavy coral surrounded by sand and sea grass between Islamorada and Marathon in the Keys. The depth ranges from 18 to 100 feet. (24°22'N 80°53'W).

Sportfishing is going strong in the Keys along the flats on the Atlantic and Gulf sides for bonefish, permit and tarpon. Bonefish stick to the shallow flats while permit and tarpon can be found along flats, in channels and around bridges. For trout and redfish, fish the back country along Florida Bay.

The lower gulf coast offers good tarpon fishing in the deep bays and passes. Trout frequent the grass flats. For redfish, try the creeks and over the bars. Mangrove snapper and sheepshead are in holes and around bridges and can be coaxed out and about with live shrimp.

Sarasota offers some good offshore fishing for king and Spanish mackerel and bluefish. A good spot is just a few miles west of Sarasota in 30 feet of water. The bottom is made of sand and shell and has high rock formations. (27°12'N 82°41'W).

Upper gulf fishing is usually good for grouper along the offshore reefs and rock piles near Steinhatchee, Horseshoe Beach, Cedar Key, Crystal River, Bayport and Homosassa River.

Panama City's Spawning Grounds is a popular spot. This flat, hard sand bottom is heavily fished for red snapper. (29°45'N 85°36'W).

For cobia, try the offshore reefs, but for rock fish try the inshore reefs. Trout hit best along the grass flats while pompano and whiting stick to the surf. Take to the piers for spadefish. For tarpon, fish the bays and inshore waters.

Snook are still out of the game in July. If you catch one, let it go.

AUGUST

This is a good month for bottom fishing along the upper Atlantic coast, especially for red snapper and grouper. A good spot is the East Ridge, about 20 miles off Daytona Beach in 13 to 14 fathoms. The bottom is a rock reef that runs parallel to the 60-foot contour cliffs. (29°13'N 80°31'W).

Inlet fishing is good for trout, redfish and flounder. All three will hit on live shrimp and fingerling mullet. Live pigfish are good bait for trout and redfish. Jigs, grubs and other artificials are good lures for trout and reds.

The lower east coast offers good offshore trolling for sailfish, dolphin, king mackerel, cobia, wahoo, false albacore and blackfin tuna. Some swordfish are still landed at night. Head boats and drift boats are available at most major ports in the area for mutton, yellowtail and red snapper and grouper. A good site for these fish is off Atlantic

Boulevard just north of Fort Lauderdale along the edge of the third reef. It is slightly broken and has heavy coral growth in 100- to 150-foot water. (26°14'N 80°03'W).

Fishing in the Keys is best during early morning and late evening hours. Fish rarely feed during the heat of the day. Go to the flats on either side of the Keys for bonefish. Fish the channels and back country for snook (although they must be released in August, too), trout, reds and permit.

Offshore reefs along the keys offer anglers some good catches of grouper and yellowtail, mangrove and mutton snapper. Tarpon are still frequenting the deeper bays and passes along the lower gulf coast while trout hug the grass flats and reds stay close to oyster bars, bridges and passes.

Some good bottom fishing can be found about 20 miles offshore along the coast off Naples. Snapper and grouper congregate here. For red and mutton snapper and red and black grouper, try fishing the 24- to 29-fathom depths where the bottom is an extensive area of sand and shell. (25°00'N 82° 46'W).

Farther up the coast, the Tampa Bay area offers redfish and sea trout in the channels, the edges of grass flats and in the passes. Tarpon hang out along the beaches and offshore.

The northern section of the gulf has some good cobia fishing around the buoys and most any other structure. In the grass flats, trout will hit surface lures early, just after daybreak. Redfish are around the offshore rock piles and oyster bars.

Tarpon Springs has some good grouper fishing 15 miles offshore in 80- to 85-foot water. A flat bottom with scattered rocks, shell and coral growth offers good living quarters for grouper. (28°98'N 83°27'W).

August is the peak month for red snapper and assorted bottom fish along the northwest gulf coast. Party boats depart daily for offshore fishing reefs from most ports. About 15 miles south of Destin is a large area for red and vermillion snapper, porgies and gag grouper in 22 to 32 fathoms. The sand bottom has 6- to 12-foot holes. A few airplane wrecks are also scattered through the area. (29°27' to 30°04'N 86°12' to 86°33'W).

Inshore fishing is best for pompano and whiting in the surf and for sea trout on the grass flats. For spadefish, try fishing off the piers. For tarpon, go to the bays and along the shore. Offshore fishing is good for king mackerel, sailfish, dolphin and blue and white marlin.

SEPTEMBER

This is the month that redfish and sea trout start moving into the rivers and inlets along the upper east coast. In the surf, you will find whiting, pompano and flounder. For tarpon, go to the inlets and sounds. Offshore, king mackerel, Spanish mackerel, cobia, sailfish and dolphin hit trolled baits. Grouper and snapper also hit along the offshore reefs along the ocean bottom. For bottom fishing, use cut bait, squid and live baitfish. The Party Grounds off Daytona Beach and Pelican Flats off Port Canaveral are two good areas for bottom fishing and trolling. The Steeples and 8-A Reef are other popular sites near Port Canaveral.

Another Party Grounds area is about 10 miles off Port Canaveral and is a good spot to find red and gag grouper, red snapper, triggerfish and grunt. The bottom is a small cliff about a half-mile long with a 6-foot drop. (28°27'N 80°17'W).

Southeast of Fort Pierce along the lower east coast, another good fishing site is a shipwreck in 50-foot water. Dolphin, barracuda, king mackerel and bonito often can be found here. The bottom is rock and it drops to 100 feet. (27°23'N 80°03'W). Fishermen also will find other offshore fish along the southeast coast, including wahoo, false albacore, sailfish, blackfin tuna, cobia, mutton, yellowtail and red snapper and grouper.

Along the Intracoastal Waterway, tarpon and sea trout hit along the flats and bridges. Sheepshead and mangrove snapper prefer to feed along the piers and bridges. Bluefish and snook usually hit better in the surf. Some croaker offer good angling along inland waters.

Angling in the Florida Keys is good, especially after a tropical storm has passed through and cleared the waters. Bonefish hit on both the Gulf and the Atlantic sides of the Keys. Along the reefs you will find grouper and mangrove, mutton and yellowtail snapper. Dol-phin can be found in the Gulf Stream and tarpon in the channels and around bridges. Go to the back country for snook, trout and redfish. The Florida Bay area is the best site during September.

Along the lower gulf coast is an excellent site — called 245 degrees from Stump Pass — for red and gag grouper, sea bass and grunt. The area has a flat sand and shell bottom with one rocky area. (26°45'N 82°35'W).

Tarpon are still hitting offshore and along the coast. Mackerel frequent the beaches. Redfish and trout can be found in the passes and around bridges.

On the upper gulf coast, redfish hang around the oyster bars to feed. A good way to catch them is to troll as close to the edge of the bars as possible with a slow, wobbling spoon rig.

The grass flats are the best sites to find sea trout. Sheepshead can be found around bars and inshore rock piles. For cobia, try the inshore reefs and around buoys and other structures. They will hit jigs tipped with shrimp, live bait and some lures. Offshore fishing is best for grouper, bluefish and king and Spanish mackerel along the upper gulf coast.

An excellent site for bluefish, mackerel and cobia on the northwest gulf coast is the wreck of the battleship USS Massachusetts, which is partially exposed on a sand ridge off Pensacola. (87°18.7'W 39°17.7'N).

OCTOBER

This is one of the top fishing months of the year. As the water cools, fish become more active as they move inshore. Fishing picks up along inland waterways, at inlets and along offshore reefs for trolling and bottom-fishing enthusiasts.

Along the east coast, some big redfish show up, especially in the northern portion of Mosquito Lagoon, Ponce Inlet between Daytona Beach and New Smyrna Beach and to the south around Sebastian Inlet. Also, bluefish are active in the surf along beaches and around fishing piers. Large sea trout in the Banana and Indian rivers and Mosquito Lagoon move from grass flats to deeper water as the weather cools and lowers water temperatures. The best fishing for drum is off bridges and piers. For tasty pompano, fish the surf with clams and sand crabs.

Also present in the surf and along the beaches are tarpon. You can also find the silver kings in the inlets as well. Few thrills can compare with hooking into a hundred-pound tarpon and watching it skyrocket into the air. Offshore trolling is good in October for king mackerel and bottom fishing is good for red snapper and grouper. Head boats are popular this time of year for anglers who enjoy going out and doing some bottom fishing for grouper, snapper and assorted bottom fish. For about $50 a day, an angler can enjoy a full day of fishing with everything but the food furnished, and some boats sell that. While half-day boats also are available, they don't go as far offshore.

Others prefer trolling the offshore reefs during October. Charter boats are popular and some anglers pitch in and split the cost of a charter that can run from $400 to $700 a day. These boats, which usually will take as many as six anglers on a trip, furnish rods, reels, tackle, bait, fighting chairs and even a mate to do the work and assist with boating, gaffing, or tagging and releasing the fish.

Offshore trolling is good along the lower east coast for sailfish, marlin, amberjack, little tunny, wahoo, cobia and both king and Spanish mackerel. Drift fishing or anchoring along the offshore reefs is good for grouper, snapper, bluefish, mackerel and pompano.

Inland waters offer anglers good fishing for sheepshead, drum, flounder, grunts, croakers, mackerel, redfish, ladyfish, snook and trout. Surf fishing is best for whiting, bluefish, pompano and croakers.

Fishing is excellent in the Keys. In the Gulf Stream, look for sailfish, wahoo, dolphin, king mackerel, tuna, bonito and African pompano. Along the wrecks and reefs, amberjack abound. Inshore, bluefish are plentiful. Cobia frequent the passes and bridges. Jack crevalle, an excellent fighter but not good eating, can be found all over. Try the reefs for jewfish — the big ones settle in small holes and around bridges. Trout and redfish hit best in the channels, in the passes, around bridges at night and in the back country.

The lower gulf coast area offers good fishing in an area called "West of Redfish Pass," which is noted for king and Spanish mackerel, bluefish and black grouper. The bottom is a 40- to 45-foot sandy area with scattered patches of flat rock (26°33'N 82°21'W).

Inshore fishing is best for snook in the rivers, canals and bays. Tarpon fishing is good also in the bays and rivers. Sea trout are found along the grass flats, around bridges and in canals. Mangrove snapper, sheepshead and redfish are in the passes, around sand bars and up in the creeks. Whiting and silver trout hit best around bridges.

Upper gulf coast fishing is excellent because the redfish start appearing in number in the creeks and rivers that empty into the Gulf of Mexico. Appearing with them are trout, mangrove snapper, sheepshead, ladyfish and jack crevalle. A choice site for reds is Bob Sikes Cut through St. George Island. Offshore fishing is good in this area and along both coasts for snapper and grouper.

Along the northwest gulf coast, blue marlin, white marlin and sailfish offer productive angling. The Panama City area is one of the top billfish offshore angling spots, especially for white marlin.

Inshore fishing is excellent during the month for redfish and sea trout as they move into the bays and rivers, and for bluefish that can be found in the surf. The scrappy blues will go after almost anything you offer them, but they seem to prefer fresh mullet cut in strips. Use a wire leader when fishing for blues or their sharp teeth will cut your line.

October is also one of the most comfortable months to fish. However, it can get windy, which may limit offshore fishing as seas kick up. Keep an eye on the weather and don't venture offshore on rough days. Instead, find a sheltered area and fish inshore.

NOVEMBER

Along the upper east coast, redfish and trout move into the inlets, lagoons and river. Mangrove snapper, sheepshead, flounder and croaker can be found in the rivers, creeks and inlets. Whiting hit best in the surf and off piers. Offshore fishing is good for king and Spanish mackerel and grouper.

The lower east coast offers good trolling in the Gulf Stream for sailfish, marlin, tuna, little tunny, skipjack and dolphin. Offshore angling is also good for bluefish, cobia, wahoo, Spanish and king mackerel. Drift boats catch lots of snapper and grouper during the month along the offshore reefs.

The Golf Ball Water Tower east of Juno Beach is an excellent site for king mackerel, mutton and vermillion snapper and grouper. It has a rugged reef bottom with heavy growth in 75- to 240-foot water. The site is also an excellent spot

for big "smoker" king mackerel and sailfish (26°32'N 79°59'W).

Some of the best inshore fishing is for drum, grunts, croakers, bluefish, pompano, Spanish mackerel, ladyfish, snook and sea trout.

The Keys offer good offshore fishing, especially in the Gulf Stream where trolling boats catch African pompano, blackfin tuna, barracuda, dolphin, sailfish and wahoo. King mackerel fishing improves in November along both coasts and bonefish can be caught on both sides of the Keys along the flats. For redfish, snook and trout, go to the Florida Bay back country. Around the offshore wrecks and reefs and inside the passes are good sites for grouper, jewfish and amberjack. For permit, fish the flats, around the bridges and in the passes.

Upper gulf coast fishing is good for redfish (channel bass) as they congregate in deep holes of the many rivers in this area along with trout, mangrove snapper and sheepshead. When the weather is cool, trout and redfish can be found in large numbers in the St. Marks River and Spring Creek in Wakulla County. Offshore angling is best for grouper, which are found most frequently over inshore rock piles.

The northwest coast is good for sailfish that move in close to shore and remain until cool water forces them to follow the current south. November is a good time to fish for red snapper and grouper. Trout, blue- and redfish angling is best in the bays and rivers. Sheepshead and mangrove snapper move into the bays and rivers also to offer some fun fishing and tasty eating.

DECEMBER

Along the upper east coast, offshore fishing is limited mostly to snapper and grouper. Party boats leave most ports daily for bottom-fishing ventures when weather and seas permit. Whether or not the boats leave port is also determined by the number of anglers wanting to fish.

One of the good spots for grouper and red and vermillion snapper is an area along Florida's east coast between St. Augustine and Daytona Beach called Long John. It is offshore in 13 to 14 fathoms along a bottom where a ridge of rock forms a steep cliff.

Closer in, whiting hit well in the surf, while trout, reds, flounder and croaker feed more in the rivers and inlets. Pilings and docks are favorite haunts for sheepshead. Use fiddler crabs or live shrimp to entice them.

This is the month for sailfish and king mackerel along the lower east coast. Both will hit offshore trolling rigs of balao and skirts. Also, both species will hit live baitfish. Bottom fishing is good during December along the offshore reefs for grouper, snapper and assorted bottom fish. A good site for red grouper, vermillion snapper and triggerfish is about 10 miles southeast of Port Canaveral in 35- to 50-fathom water where a ridge of irregular rock lies parallel to the 100-fathom curve. (28°00'N 80°00'W).

Surf fishing is good for whiting, croaker, bluefish and pompano along the east coast. Spotted sea trout, silver trout, bluefish and snook prefer the inland waters during the cold months of the year.

Angling in the Keys is good for king mackerel, sailfish, tuna, amberjack and dolphin. Also there are usually fewer fisherman during December and an abundance of fish. Offshore angling is good for other species as well, including African pompano, barracuda, little tunny, blackfin tuna and grouper.

Inshore Keys fishing is good for bonefish in the ocean, bayside grass and sand flats. Cobia and jewfish hit around reefs, passes and bridges. Snook and redfish stay inside the back country. Sea trout are active on the bayside grass and flats. Shrimp is good bait for most of the inshore fish.

The lower gulf coast offers some good grouper and red snapper fishing, especially along the 40-fathom contour some 30 to 40 miles offshore. One of the favorites for scamp, red, yelloweye and mutton snapper is Hambone Ridges situated in 30- to 50-fathom water. The bottom is a series of well-defined ridges on a flat, sandy bottom (25°12' to 25°40'N 83° 06'W). Trolling boats concentrate on king mackerel fishing along this area.

Inshore, fishermen go after snook as they move into rivers and bays. Others go for sea trout that are in the canals and around bridges. Spanish mackerel move along the beaches. Redfish stick to the passes. Whiting can be caught around bridges and silver trout are on the flats and around the bridges.

A small — but good — area for grouper is on the gulf coast between Tarpon Springs and Homosassa River. About 15 miles offshore in 65- to 70-foot water, this spot has 14 ledges situated on a sand and shell bottom (28°33'N 83°06'W).

Inshore inside the rivers and creeks, fishing is best for trout, redfish, sheepshead, mangrove snapper and jack crevalle. Reds and sea trout move into Crystal River and Homosassa River as well as other rivers during cold snaps when water temperatures drop. Mangrove snapper fishing is good in the deep holes of the rivers, especially around rocky bottoms and river shores.

Fishing slows along the northwest gulf coast. Party boats usually run only on weekends for dedicated anglers in search of grouper and snapper. A good spot for bottom fishing is the Mud Banks area about 40 miles off Panama City. In 31 to 34 fathoms, the area's bottom has a rock ledge that drops 3 to 4 fathoms and extends 7 to 8 miles (29°22'N 85°45' to 85°55'W).

Inshore fishing is good for trout around springs and rivers. Redfish, on the other hand, prefer the surf and bars inside the rivers and in the bays. Surf fishing is good for whiting and bluefish.

December is one of the best months for sailfishing in the Stuart-Fort Pierce area. The best sailfishing day I've had was a cold and windy Dec. 31 when my sons and I raised 19 sailfish. Each of us managed to catch and release one.

AN OVERVIEW

Here is a brief listing of fish anglers will more than likely encounter in each area of the state:

Northeast Atlantic Coast: Surf casting for redfish, bluefish and drum. Inside bays and inlets best for sea trout, redfish, blues, drum and tarpon.

Central East Coast: Trout, redfish are in the surf and inshore. So are jack crevalle, drum and tripletail (around buoys, too). Fish lower areas for sailfish and snook.

Lower East Coast: Sailfishing is done in the entire area, especially at Stuart and Palm Beach. Gulf Stream has sailfish, marlin, mako shark, dolphin and tuna. Shoreline best for snook, tarpon, sea trout, and mackerel during runs.

Florida Keys: Upper Keys good for trout, snapper, redfish and especially bonefish, permit and tarpon. Other good Keys fishing for wahoo, grouper, amberjack and barracuda.

Northwest Gulf Coast: Noted for red snapper, flounder, grouper, cobia, blue runners and trout.

Upper Gulf Coast: Summer fishing is best for trout, redfish, grouper, flounder and tarpon. Fall is good for mangrove snapper and spring offers offshore runs of cobia and king mackerel.

Middle Gulf Coast: This area is noted for tarpon from Homosassa River to Boca Grande. Snook, cobia and trout are popular along with king and Spanish mackerel. Offshore is best for grouper and jack crevalle.

Lower Gulf Coast: Best for tarpon, snook, redfish, pompano and mackerel during runs.

Note: Remember to check with a Marine Patrol officer or the Department of Natural Resources about local laws governing fishing in your area.

3

HOW TO RIG BAITS

A sharp hook is most important when fishing. Many big ones get away because of a rusty or dull hook. It's also important that you know where to put the hook in the bait. For instance, if you hook a live shrimp through the dark spot in its head, you will surely be fishing with a dead shrimp. Make the bait look natural, whether it's dead and rigged for trolling, or live bait to be used for inshore or offshore angling. A live fingerling mullet hooked through both lips looks natural as it swims through the water and, thus, will attract fish.

When trolling balao, whole mullet, strip bait and other baits offshore for marlin, sailfish, wahoo, dolphin and other bluewater fish, you should rig your baits to skip naturally across the surface. Or, if used on downriggers or planers, the baits should emulate a live baitfish swimming at various depths.

Here are some suggestions on how to hook and rig baits for offshore, pier, surf, inlet and other types of angling:

Shrimp: Hook shrimp through the head or tail. Hooking it through the head is the most popular method. Avoid hooking it through the dark spot in the head. Peel fresh shrimp and hook from head to tail on the underside. Shrimp pieces may also be used for bottom fishing.

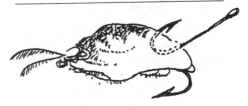

Sand flea: Also known as a sand crab, scud, mole crab and sand bug, this is a popular bait for surf fishing. Hook it through the middle of the antennae and through the center of the body so that the hook comes out the rear pointing down. Another way is to hook it from the rear underside with the hook pointing upward.

Mullet: When fishing with live mullet, hook the mullet through both lips from the bottom lip upward through the top lip. For trolling:

1. Cut hole here and remove backbone with deboner. Stitch hole closed.

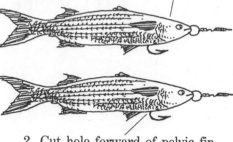

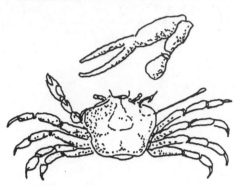

Fiddler crab: Remove claws and insert hook in claw hole. Thread upward through outer part of shell.

2. Cut hole forward of pelvic fin, remove insides, insert hook shank.

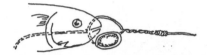

3. For deep trolling, attach lead. For best swimming action, scale bait and smash head flat.

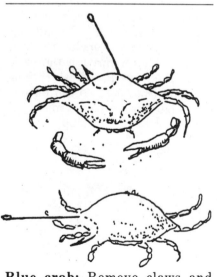

Blue crab: Remove claws and thread the hook carefully. Don't split the shell.

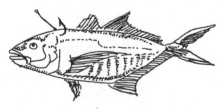

Blue runner: Use single hook rig for slow trolling with or without outrigger or from a kite (yes, the kind you fly). Blue runner is good for bottom fishing when cut into chunks or strips. Hook cut bait through the flesh and out through the skin.

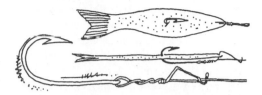

Strip bait: This is mainly used for trolling, but it can be cast and retrieved. Use bait with tough skin and oily flesh: bonito, mackerel, balao, menhaden and mullet. Scale, remove bones, run hook through flesh and out through the skin.

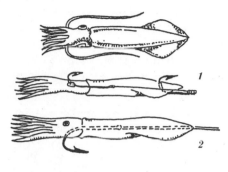

1

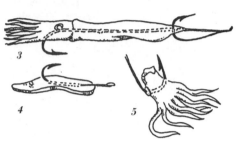

2

3

4   *5*

Squid: Illustrations 1 and 2 are squid-rigged trolling baits. Illustrations 3, 4 and 5 are bottom-fishing squid rigs.

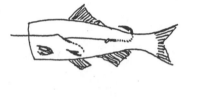

Herring:

1. Cut plug "mooching" rig. Remove head with sharp knife at a slant from back to belly and slightly rearward. Remove insides.

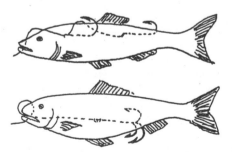

2. Whole bait fish rigged for other types of fishing may be jigged (mooched).

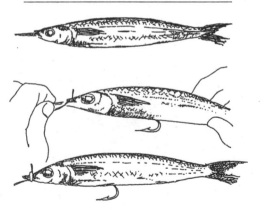

Balao: The balao (pronounced bal-lyho) is probably the most effective offshore trolling bait used in Florida waters. Breaking off its long lower beak and wiring its mouth together makes it more effective and enables it to swim through the water naturally. Used with a Sea Witch, it is a deadly combination for sailfish, marlin, dolphin, king mackerel, and almost all species of bluewater fish.

Popping cork: A popular rig for trout and redfish, the popping cork with live shrimp is used along the grass flats and sand bars. This noise-maker is a sure way to entice spotted sea trout and reds. The rig consists of a long bobber, a split shot, hook and shrimp.

Barracuda double: This double hook rig is an effective way to double your chances with barracuda and other fish when trolling. Run the point of your first hook through the eye of a second hook. Then you have a double hook rig.

Feather and strip combo: This offshore trolling combination makes a great rig for king mackerel, bonito and other ocean fighters. Simply hook a piece of strip bait on a feather jig.

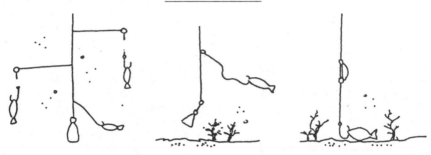

Bottom rigs: The three illustrations show the varied ways for bottom-rigging. The first rig is used when fishing for fish near the bottom. The leader and hook can be moved up or down as needed. The second illustration shows another favorite method of rigging for bottom fish. The third is good except for sheepshead and a few other nibblers that are hard to feel.

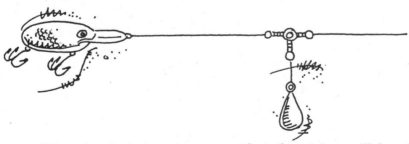

Deep trolling rig: A three-point swivel or "T" is used as illustrated. Line connects to one point, the leader to another and the sinker to the third. Lightweight line is used so that the sinker will break if snagged on the bottom. The bait will stand a better chance of riding over the snag or rock, thus sparing the angler time and frustration.

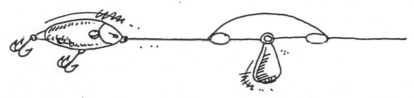

Trolling rig with release sinker:
This rig is used when a lot of
weight is necessary to sink the bait
to a proper level. Because a heavy
sinker will interfere with the action
when a fish strikes, this rig will release the sinker when the fish hits.
Make two slip knots with light line
and attach the sinker to the light
line. When the fish strikes, the line
will break, the slip knots will come
loose and the sinker will drop off.

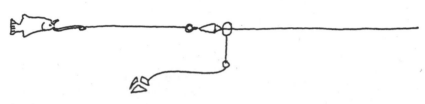

Fish finder: Line is free to run
through double-eye swivel, passing
through the eye and attached to a
leather thong. The leader is attached to the opposite side of the
thong. The sinker drops from the
swivel eye and slides freely as far
as the thong. Even cautious fish
will fall for this bait because there
is far less drag on the bait.

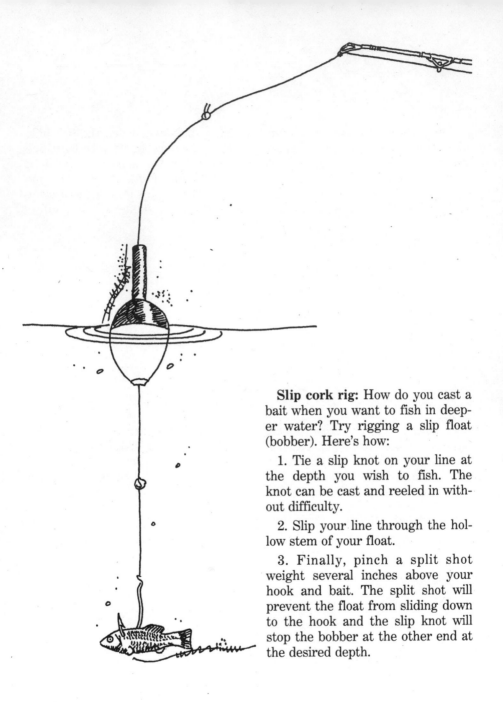

Slip cork rig: How do you cast a bait when you want to fish in deeper water? Try rigging a slip float (bobber). Here's how:

1. Tie a slip knot on your line at the depth you wish to fish. The knot can be cast and reeled in without difficulty.

2. Slip your line through the hollow stem of your float.

3. Finally, pinch a split shot weight several inches above your hook and bait. The split shot will prevent the float from sliding down to the hook and the slip knot will stop the bobber at the other end at the desired depth.

4

TYING KNOTS

S trong knots and good fishing line are important, even critical, to successful fishing ventures. There's nothing quite so disconcerting as hooking into a large fish only to have it make a lunge and snap the line. Some saltwater anglers change their lines after each trip. Others, after a few trips. At the very least, the salt should be washed from the lines with fresh water after each outing.

Never store line in hot places or in sunlight. Both will cause it to weaken. Another line tip: When tying simple knots, it's a good idea to wet the line so that the knot will tie more smoothly. Pull tightly when tying knots. If you don't, a big fish may, and break the line in the process.

Some knots that may come in handy when rigging for heavy-duty offshore fishing or for lighter inshore angling follow. Descriptions are courtesy of the International Game Fish Association.

IMPROVED CLINCH KNOT

1. Run end of line through the eye of the hook or lure.

2. Loop around the standing part of the line five or six times.

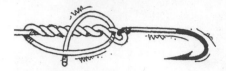 

3. Thread the tag end (the part of the line in which the knot is tied) back between the eye and the coils as shown and then back through the hoop.

4. Pull up tightly and trim the tag end.

TRILENE KNOT

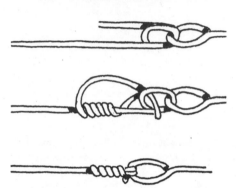

A variation of the improved clinch knot, this is an extra strong knot. Run the tag end through the eye and then run it through the double opening.

OFFSHORE SWIVEL KNOT

A knot used to attach a swivel or snap to a double line.

1. Slip the loop end of a double line through the eye of the swivel. Next, rotate the loop end a half turn to put a single twist between the loop and the swivel eye.

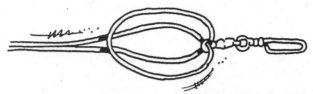

2. Pass the loop with the twist over the swivel. Hold the end of the loop, plus both legs of the double line with one hand. Then let the swivel slide to the other side of the double loops now formed.

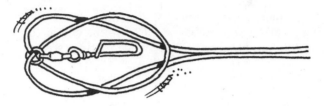

3. Still holding the loop and lines with one hand, rotate swivel through the center of both loops at least six times.

4. Continue holding both legs of double line tightly but release the end of the loop. Now, pull on swivel. Loops of line will begin to gather.

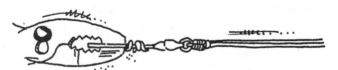

5. To draw the knot tight, grip the swivel with a pair of pliers and push the loops toward the eye with your fingers while keeping the lines of the double line pulled tightly.

BIMINI TWIST

Used for offshore trolling, this double loop is much stronger than a single line and is used for tying double lines of 5 feet or less. Two people may be needed to tie longer sections.

1. Measure just more than twice the length you want for the double line and bring the end back to the standing line and hold together. Rotate the end of the loop 20 times while putting twists in the line.

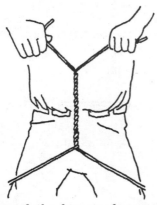

2. Spread the loop to force twists together about 10 inches below the tag end. Step both feet through the loop and bring it up around your knees to put pressure on the column of twists by spreading your knees apart.

hand with tension just slightly off the vertical position. With your other hand, move the tag end to position at right angle to twists. Keep the tension on the loop with your knees and gradually ease the tension of the tag end so it will roll over the column of twists, beginning just below the upper twist.

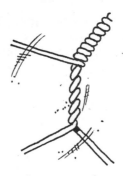

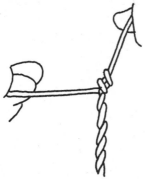

3. With twists forced tightly together, hold standing line in one

4. Spread your legs apart slowly to maintain pressure on the loop. Steer the tag end into a spiral coil as it continues to roll over twisted line.

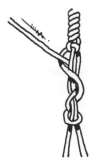

5. When the spiral of the tag end has rolled over the column of twists, continue keeping knee pressure on the loop and move your hand that has held the standing line down to grasp the knot. Next, place your finger on the line where the loop joins the knot to prevent slippage of the last turn. Now take half-hitch with the tag end around nearest leg of the loop and pull up tightly.

7. Make two more turns with the tag end around both legs of the loop, winding inside the bend of line formed by the loose half-hitch and toward the main knot. Next, pull the tag end slowly, forcing the three loops to gather in a spiral.

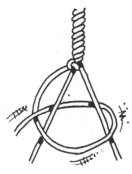

8. When the loops are pulled neatly against the main knot, tighten to lock the knot in place. Trim the tag end about a quarter inch from the knot.

6. With the half-hitch holding knot, release the knee pressure, but keep the loop stretched out tightly. Use remaining tag end and take half-hitch around both legs of the loop, but do not pull tightly.

SPIDER HITCH

While it may not be as resilient under sharp impact, the spider hitch is an easier and faster knot to form a double line. This line is just as strong as the Bimini Twist, but is not a practical knot to use on lines in the 30-pound class.

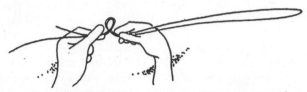

1. Form a loop of the leader length you desire. Near the point where it meets the standing line, twist a section into a small reverse loop.

2. Hold the small loop between your thumb and forefinger — thumb extended well above your finger and loop standing out beyond the end of your thumb.

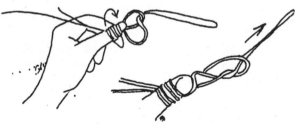

3. Next, wind the double line around both your thumb and the loop, taking five turns. Pass the remainder of the large loop through the smaller one and pull to make five turns unwind off the thumb.

4. Pull turns around the base of the loop tightly and snip off at the thumb.

5

WHAT, WHERE AND WHEN

The Florida Department of Natural Resources divides the state's coastal waters into five areas, as shown on the accompanying map. Also included in this chapter is a chart showing the best fishing for each season of the year in these areas.

Before you strike out for these areas, check the list below to discover what you'll want to take with you in the way of rods and reels, hooks, leaders and baits to catch the fish you're after.

African pompano: medium trolling, spinning; 4/0-5/0 hook, heavy monofilament line; jigs, natural baits for trolling, live bait.

Amberjack: medium, heavy spinning, casting; 4/0-5/0, 80-lb. monofilament; live bait, pinfish, etc., jigs.

Barracuda: light to medium spinning, trolling; 5/0, wire leader; spoons, live bait, tube lures.

Bluefish: surfcasting, casting, spinning; 4/0-5/0, wire leader; cut bait, live bait, spoons.

Bonefish: light, spinning, casting; 1/0-2/0, light monofilament; jigs, shrimp, streamer flies.

Cobia: medium spinning or casting; 2/0-4/0, heavy monofilament; live bait, shrimp, mullet, jigs.

Dolphin: light to medium spinning, trolling, casting; 1/0-2/0 medium monofilament; jigs, lures, live or cut bait.

Drum: surfcasting, casting, spinning; 4/0-6/0, wire, heavy monofilament; sand crabs, shrimp, jigs, cut bait.

Flounder: light to medium casting or spinning; 2/0, medium monofilament; shrimp, cut bait.

Grouper: medium trolling, casting, heavy spinning; 3/0-8/0, heavy wire, monofilament; live or cut bait, trolled Rapalas, strips, jigs.

Grunt: light spinning, casting; 1/0-4/0, no leader; shrimp, cut bait, jigs.

Jack crevalle: medium casting, trolling, spinning; 2/0-5/0, heavy monofilament; live bait, spoons, trolled spoons.

Mackerel (cero): light; 1/0-2/0, wire leader; live bait, spoons.

Mackerel (king): heavy casting, medium trolling; 5/0-7/0, long wire; live baitfish, feathers and strips, balao, spoons, strip bait.

Mackerel (Spanish): light trolling, spinning, casting; 2/0-4/0, wire; live bait, spoons, feather and strips.

Ladyfish: light casting or spinning; 1/0, light monofilament or no leader; plugs, spoons, live bait.

Mangrove snapper: light spinning or casting; 1/0, medium monofilament; jigs, live shrimp, live baitfish.

Marlin (blue): medium to heavy trolling; 5/0, heavy monofilament or wire; whole mullet, balao and skirts, live bait.

Marlin (white): medium to heavy spinning or casting; 5/0, heavy monofilament or wire; whole mullet, strip bait, feathers.

Permit: light to medium spinning or casting; 1/0, monofilament; sand fleas, shrimp, jigs.

Pompano: light spinning and casting; 1/0-2/0, nylon; sand fleas, small spoons, jigs, streamers.

Redfish (channel bass): light to medium casting, spinning; 1/0-2/0, monofilament; live bait, spoons, jigs, plugs.

Red snapper: medium spinning, casting; 4/0-5/0, wire, heavy monofilament; live bait, cut bait, jigs.

Sailfish: medium to heavy spinning, casting; 1/0-5/0, wire; balao and skirts, whole mullet, strip bait, live bait.

Sea trout: light casting or spinning; 1/0-2/0, monofilament; live shrimp, jigs, lures, live pigfish.

Sheepshead: light spinning or casting; 1/0-3/0, heavy monofilament; fiddler crabs, hermit crabs, sand fleas, shrimp.

Snook: medium to heavy casting or spinning; 2/0-4/0, heavy monofilament leader; live bait, shrimp, jigs, bucktails, plugs, streamers, spoons.

Tarpon: medium to heavy spinning or casting; 4/0-7/0, heavy monofilament or wire; live bait, dead bait, jigs, artificial lures.

Tripletail: medium casting, spinning; 1/0-3/0, monofilament or wire; live bait, plugs, jigs.

Wahoo: medium casting, spinning; 1/0-3/0, wire; strip bait, balao and skirt, boned mullet, jigs.

Whiting: light casting, spinning; 1-1/0, monofilament; shrimp, sand fleas, jigs.

Yellowtail snapper: light to medium spinning, casting; 1/0-2/0, heavy monofilament or wire; shrimp, cut bait, live bait, jigs.

Tuna (blackfin): medium trolling; 3/0, wire or monofilament; trolled small lures, small rigged baits.

Tuna (bluefin): heavy trolling; 5/0, heavy monofilament or wire; whole rigged mullet.

Tuna (yellowfin): medium to heavy trolling; 5/0, wire; trolled strip bait, balao, mullet, artificials.

AREA 1

Spring	Summer	Fall	Winter
Amberjack	Amberjack	Amberjack	Redfish
Barracuda	Marlin	Marlin	Sheepshead
Cobia	Bonito	Sailfish	Grouper
Bluefish	Sailfish	Dolphin	Snapper
King mackerel	Dolphin	Barracuda	Sea trout
Pompano	Barracuda	Sea trout	Drum
Sea trout	King mackerel	Sheepshead	Bluefish
Sheepshead	Tarpon	Spanish mackerel	
Red snapper	Cobia	Redfish	
Grouper	Flounder	Drum	
Redfish	Sea trout	Grouper	
	Spanish mackerel	Snapper	
	Grouper	Cobia	
	Red snapper	Flounder	
	Snapper	Bluefish	

AREA 2

Spring	Summer	Fall	Winter
King mackerel	Spanish mackerel	King mackerel	Sheepshead
Dolphin	Sea trout	Sea trout	Sea trout
Cobia	Cobia	Flounder	Grouper
Pompano	Snook	Bluefish	Snapper
Sea trout	Flounder	Drum	
Bluefish	Redfish	Grouper	
Redfish	Tarpon	Snapper	
Mangrove snapper	Grouper	Snook	
Sheepshead	Snapper	Tarpon	
Spanish mackerel	Mangrove snapper	Mangrove snapper	
Barracuda	Permit	Redfish	
Snook	Barracuda		
Tarpon			
Grouper			
Snapper			

AREA 3

Spring	Summer	Fall	Winter
Amberjack	Amberjack	Sailfish	Sailfish
Bonito	Dolphin	Dolphin	Dolphin
Dolphin	Sailfish	Wahoo	Wahoo
Sailfish	Bonefish	Marlin	Marlin
Wahoo	Sea trout	Bonefish	Barracuda
Bonefish	Barracuda	Redfish	Redfish
Cobia	Tarpon	Tarpon	Tarpon
Flounder	Snook	Snook	Snook
Sea trout	Cero mackerel	Amberjack	Cobia
Redfish	Spanish mackerel	Sea trout	Mangrove snapper
Snook	Flounder	King mackerel	Bonefish
Tarpon	Permit	Spanish mackerel	Sea trout
Grouper	Redfish	Grouper	Grouper
Snapper	Grouper	Cobia	Snapper
Pompano	Snapper	Mangrove snapper	Blackfin tuna
King mackerel	Cobia	Flounder	Cero mackerel
Spanish mackerel	Bonito	Sheepshead	Sheepshead
Barracuda	Wahoo		Spanish mackerel
Blackfin tuna	Bluefish		
Bluefish	Blackfin tuna		

AREA 4

Spring	Summer	Fall	Winter
Sailfish	Sailfish	Sailfish	Sailfish
Dolphin	Dolphin	Dolphin	Dolphin
Wahoo	Amberjack	Wahoo	Wahoo
Barracuda	Barracuda	Bluefish	Barracuda
King mackerel	Spanish mackerel	King mackerel	Blackfin tuna
Sea trout	Sea trout	Sea trout	Sea trout
Sheepshead	Whiting	Sheepshead	Redfish
Bluefish	Snook	Bluefish	Bonito
Spanish mackerel	Pompano	Redfish	Sheepshead
Redfish		Snook	
Tripletail		Spanish mackerel	
Snook		Whiting	
Grouper			
Snapper			
Drum			

AREA 5

Spring	Summer	Fall	Winter
Sailfish	Sailfish	Sailfish	Sailfish
Bluefish	Amberjack	Drum	Drum
Pompano	Bonito	Flounder	Flounder
Sheepshead	Dolphin	King mackerel	Bluefish
Sea trout	Bluefish	Spanish mackerel	Redfish
Grouper	King mackerel	Sheepshead	Sheepshead
Snapper	Spanish mackerel	Sea trout	Sea trout
	Tarpon	Redfish	Grouper
	Grouper	Snapper	Snapper
	Snapper	Grouper	
	Flounder		

6

RULES AND REGULATIONS

lorida's fishing regulations are constantly changing to protect various species of endangered fish — especially redfish, sea trout, mackerel, cobia, amberjack, grouper, snapper, snook and tarpon. Blackened redfish, a popular Cajun dish, has put commercial pressure on reds. Snook have felt pressure from recreational anglers, pollution, loss of habitat to construction and freezes that have killed thousands of the linesiders. The snook has made a dramatic comeback, though, since closed seasons were imposed several years ago. Those seasons remain to ensure the snook's survival during January and February, when cold weather makes it sluggish and therefore vulnerable, and during the spawning season June through August.

Size limits also have been placed on snook and redfish. Snook must be at least 24 inches long. There is a total possession limit and daily bag limit of two fish, only one of which may be 34 inches or longer.

The Marine Fisheries Commission still is considering size and number limits on other species.

For information on any changes in coastal fishing regulations, and to inquire about information not listed in this chapter, contact your nearest Florida Marine Patrol office. Locations and phone numbers are listed at the end of this chapter. Federal regulations may vary from state regulations.

TAKING IT TO THE LIMIT

(Note: Fork size limit is from nose tip to rear center edge of tail. Overall length is from nose tip to tail tip.)

Bluefish: Minimum size limit to fork of tail is 10 inches; no bag limits on the number that can be caught and kept.

Bonefish: Minimum fork limit, 18 inches; bag limit, 1; possession limit, 1.

Cobia: Minimum fork size, 33 inches; possession limit, 2.

Flounder: Minimum fork limit, 11 inches; no bag or possession limits.

Grouper: Minimum size overall, 20 inches; no maximum size limit; bag limit, 5; possession limit, 10. This includes red, black, Nassau, gag and yellowfin grouper. Red hind and rock hind grouper are exempt from limits.

King Mackerel: Minimum size, 12 inches. The bag limit is two fish, but the bag limit in the Gulf-Atlantic fishery is reduced to one fish when federal waters close to all harvests. Check with the nearest Marine Patrol office for closed seasons.

Black mullet: 50 per vessel or person, whichever is less.

Permit: You can keep only two permit 20 inches or longer. There is no bag limit on fish measuring less than 20 inches.

Pompano: Must be 10 inches or longer on the fork size; no bag limit.

Redfish (Red drum): Minimum overall size, 18 inches; maximum size limit, 27 inches; bag limit, 1. Closed season: March, April, May.

Billfish: Anglers are allowed to keep one billfish per day, including sailfish, marlin and spearfish. These species cannot be bought or sold. Sailfish must have a minimum length of 57 inches. Blue marlin must measure 86 inches and white marlin must be a minimum 62 inches in length. There is no size limit on spearfish.

Spanish mackerel: Fork size limit, 12 inches; daily bag limit, 5.

Sea bass: Minimum size overall, 8 inches; no bag or possession limits.

Spotted sea trout: Minimum fork size, 14 inches; maximum, 24 inches. Only one sea trout over 24 inches may be kept. Bag limit is 10 per day.

Snapper: Anglers are allowed to keep two red snapper per day and they must be a minimum of 13 inches long. Schoolmaster snapper must be 10 inches minimum length and fishermen may keep 10 per day. Gray (mangrove) snapper must be at least 10 inches long also, but anglers are allowed to keep only five fish per day. Lane and vermillion snapper must be eight inches long and there is no possession limit on these species. All other snapper must be 12 inches in total length. Anglers can have an aggregate of 10 snapper that have a bag limit. Also included are blackfin, cubera, dog, mahogany, mutton, queen, silk and yellowtail.

Snook: Minimum size overall, 24 inches; but only one snook 34 inches or longer can be kept. Daily bag limit, 2; possession limit, 2. Closed seasons: January, February, June, July and August.

Striped bass: Because of its migration in and out of the sea, the striped bass may be found in fresh water or saltwater. It is rarely caught in Florida saltwater. Effective March 1, 1988, control was turned over to the Florida Game and Fresh Water Fish Commission, and a new regulation on striped, sunshine and white bass went into effect. An aggregate daily limit of 20 and a possession limit of 40 is permitted. No more than six fish can be 24 inches or longer.

Tarpon: Catch and release is encouraged. If you want to keep a tarpon, you must buy in advance a

$50 tarpon tag and have it in your possession when a tarpon is caught.

When fishing for snook, redfish, grouper, all snapper, sea trout, pompano, Spanish mackerel, lobster, cobia, black drum or amberjack, do not dress them before returning to shore. They must be whole when you return so that your fish can be measured and identified if you're stopped. It's hard to identify a fish fillet. It's also impossible to get accurate measurements. The burden of proof is on the angler, and there are stiff fines for cleaning these fish before returning to shore.

While bag limits sometimes vary outside Florida's coastal waters, if you have fish aboard your boat while in coastal waters, officials will assume you caught the fish inside Florida's coastal waters, which extend 9 nautical miles in the Gulf and 3 nautical miles in the Atlantic.

Headquarters for the Florida Marine Patrol office is in the Marjory Stoneman Douglas Building, 3900 Commonwealth Blvd., Tallahassee, Fla. 32399; telephone, (904) 488-5757. District offices follow:

Panama City Beach, (904) 233-5150; Carrabelle, (904) 697-3741; Homosassa Springs, (904) 628-6196; Tampa, (813) 272-2516; Fort Myers, (813) 332-6971; Miami, (305) 325-3346; Titusville, (407) 383-2740; Jacksonville Beach, (904) 359-6580; Marathon, (305) 289-2320; Jupiter, (407) 624-6935; Pensacola, (904) 444-8978.

Almost everyone who wants to catch saltwater fish needs a saltwater fishing license. However, there are some exceptions: anyone under 16 years old; any Florida resident fishing in saltwater from land or from a structure fixed to the land; any Florida resident 65 or older; anyone fishing from a pier which has been issued a pier saltwater fishing license; any person fishing from a boat that has a valid recreational vessel saltwater fishing license. Other exemptions include: any Florida resident who is a member of the U.S. Armed Forces and not stationed in Florida when fishing at home on leave for 30 days or less, upon submission of orders; anyone who has been accepted by the Florida Department of Health and Rehabilitative Serves and anyone who has been assigned by a court to an HRS authorized rehabilitation program involving training in Florida aquatic resources. A Florida resident who is certified as totally and permanently disabled may obtain a permanent license at no charge from a county tax collector. Finally, anyone who holds a valid commercial saltwater products license other than the owner, operator or custodian of a vessel for which a saltwater fishing license is required.

Saltwater fishing licenses are available for Florida residents (anyone who has resided in Florida continually for six months) for 10 days, one year or five years. Non-residents may buy three-day, seven-day or one-year licenses. Lifetime saltwater licenses and lifetime sportsmen's licenses are available for Florida residents. Costs for these licenses vary according to the person's age. For costs and changes in licensing rules, contact your local tax collector's office.

7

SHELLFISH REGULATIONS

Shellfish may be taken throughout Florida waters except during the closed seasons listed below. Florida lobster are actually crawfish and are referred to as such. They are among the most elusive of the sea creatures. They also are among the most succulent.

Scallops also rank at the top of the gourmet's list of seafood dishes. Many anglers put away their rods during the scallop season and snorkel or wade for the tasty bay scallops, especially along the coastal waters of the Gulf between the Crystal and Homosassa rivers and off Anclote Key near Tarpon Springs.

Some counties have limits on sport shrimping. Volusia, for example, has a 5-gallon limit per boat per night, but neighboring Brevard has no limit on the tasty crustaceans.

Closed seasons:

Crawfish: April 1-Aug. 5

Oysters: June, July and August in Dixie and Levy counties; July, August and September in all other counties.

Scallops: April 1-June 30. Special regulations apply in St. Joe Bay.

Stone crabs: May 15-Oct. 15. (Cannot possess the whole crab at any time.)

THE SPECIFICS

Bay scallops: Recreational daily bag limit is 5 gallons of whole scallops or a half gallon of shucked scallop meat per person. It is unlawful to use mechanical harvesting gear in waters less than 3 feet deep.

Blue crabs: It is illegal to use more than five traps for the taking of blue crabs without a permit from the Department of Natural Resources. Traps may be worked during daylight hours only.

Crawfish: Crawfish (lobster) must remain in a whole condition at all times while being transported on or below the waters of the state. No egg-bearing females may be taken. Egg clusters easily can be seen attached to the outside of the body. The use of grains, spears, grabs, hooks or similar devices is illegal. It also is unlawful to possess, have aboard your boat or remove from the waters of Florida within any 24-hour period more than 24 crawfish per boat without first obtaining a crawfish license. The molesting taking, or trapping of spiny lobster within Biscayne Bay-Card Sound Crawfish Sanctuary within Dade and Monroe counties is prohibited. Divers must have a carapace-measuring device in possession and must measure crawfish in water. Diver flags must be displayed while diving or snorkeling. Check with DNR for special two-day sports fishermen's season.

Hard clams: These can be taken only during daylight hours — a half hour before sunrise to a half hour after sunset. It is unlawful to take, possess or transport clams on the water at any other time. It is unlawful to use a rake, dredge or other mechanical device to harvest hard clams in any grass bed. Rakes or tongs used to take clams must have at least seven-eighths of an inch space between the teeth and seven-eighths of an inch space between bars or dividers of any basket attached. Special permit is required to use powered rakes, dredges and other mechanical devices. All vessels used in harvesting hard clams must have shade to shield clams from the sun at all times. They also must be equipped with one or more cull boards or cull racks having no less than seven-eighths of an inch clear space between the bars or other dividers. Clams may only be taken from approved shellfish harvesting areas. Check with the nearest Marine Patrol office.

Oysters: Oysters may be taken only from approved shellfish harvesting areas. For special regulations, contact your nearest Florida Marine Patrol office. Oysters must measure 3 inches. Closed seasons are June, July and August in Dixie and Levy counties and July, August and September in all other areas.

Stone crab claws: No trapping is allowed except by permit from the Department of Natural Resources. The use of spears, grains, grabs, hooks or similar devices that can puncture, crush or injure the crab body is prohibited. A claw or claws of legal size may be taken, but the crab must be released alive. It is unlawful to remove claws from egg-bearing females. The forearm of the stone crab must be 2¾ inches for legal size.

Turtles: It is unlawful to take, kill, molest, disturb, harass, mutilate, destroy or cause to be destroyed, sell, offer for sale or transfer any marine turtle, turtle nest or turtle egg.

Manta rays: It is unlawful to intentionally destroy a manta ray.

Coral: It is unlawful to take, possess or destroy sea fans, hard corals or fire corals unless it can be shown by certified invoice that it was imported from a foreign country.

Barracuda

Sea Bass

Striped Bass

Bluefish

Bonefish

Cobia

Dolphin

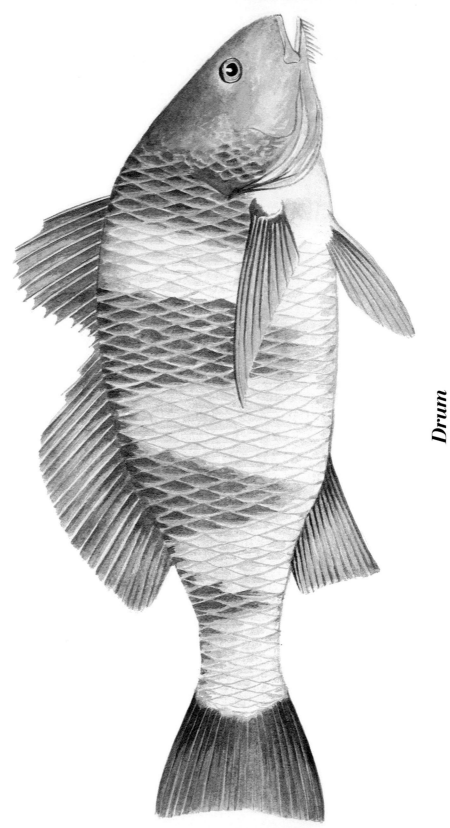

Drum

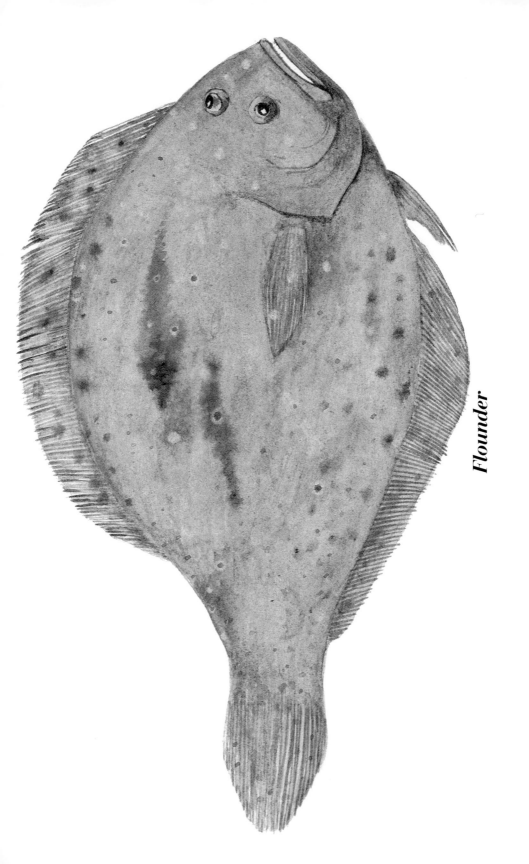

Flounder

Grouper

Jewfish

King Mackerel

Spanish Mackerel

Blue Marlin

White Marlin

Mullet

Permit

Pompano

Redfish

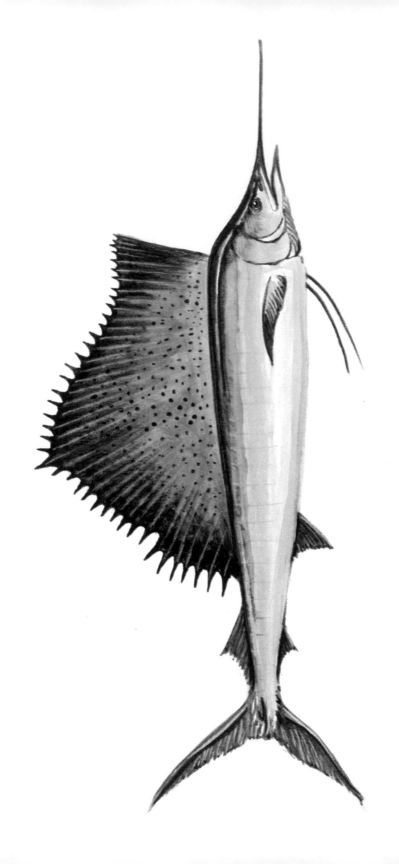

Sailfish

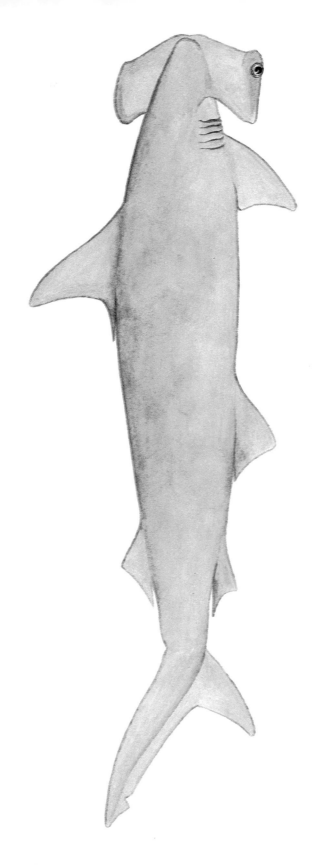

Hammerhead Shark

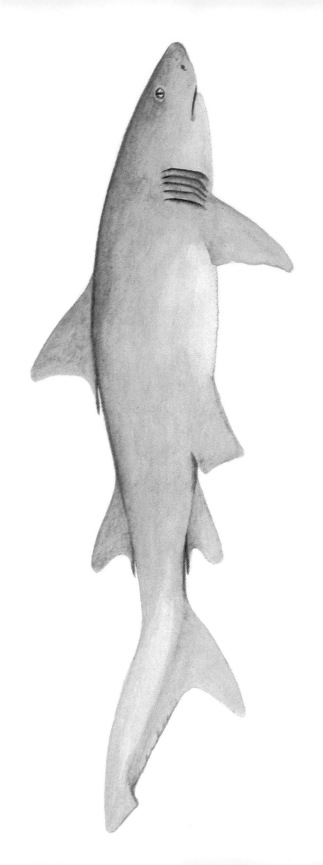

Lemon Shark

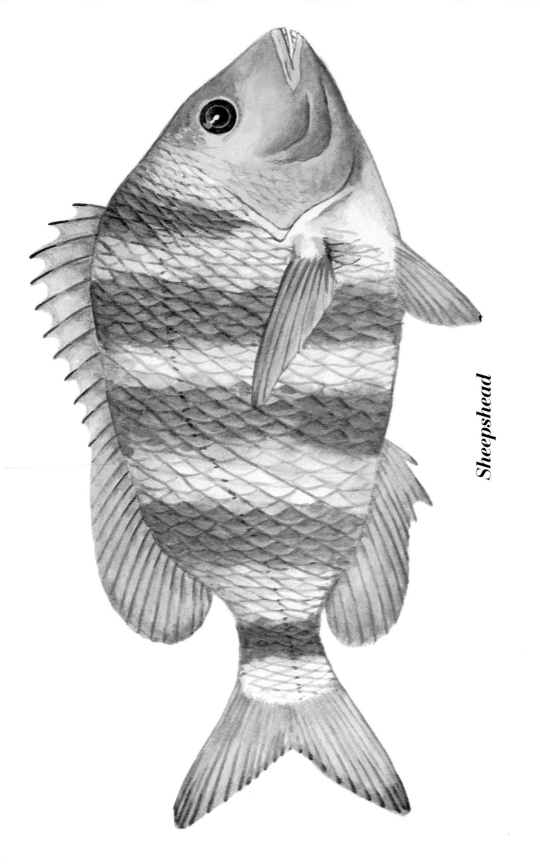

Sheepshead

Mangrove Snapper

Mutton Snapper

Red Snapper

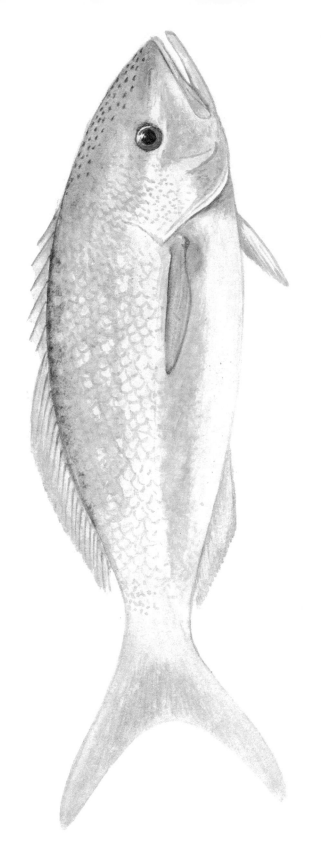

Yellowtail Snapper

Snook

Tarpon

Spotted Sea Trout

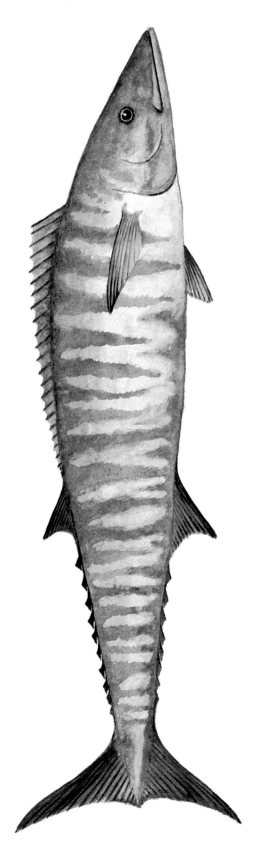

Wahoo

Whiting

CAUGHT AT
TIMMONS DOC

8

MARINAS

A longtime friend of mine, John Pitts of Orlando, complained a couple of years ago that he wanted to take his wife for a weekend outing on their boat, but that he was unable to find a listing of marinas where he could tie his boat up overnight. He also wanted to find a marina with a nice motel and restaurant located nearby. That conversation prompted me to include this chapter on marinas.

Other anglers, I'm sure, are seeking places to dock their boats for the night or weekend as they ply Florida's thousands of miles of coastal waters in search of the state's many species of gamefish.

Often, they need to refuel or to pick up some fishing and boating supplies. Groceries are available at many marinas. So are restaurants, motels and other facilities.

You may need a fishing guide or a charter boat to learn the waters. Or, perhaps you need to pick up some live bait. All of these and other conveniences are available at many of the marinas. Maybe you want to trailer your boat to the marina and use the ramp there for an ocean or inshore outing.

This list of coastal marinas and facilities has been prepared with the help of the Division of State Lands, using its most recent list of multislip marinas.

BAY COUNTY

Facility name	Telephone	Waterbody	Fuel	Live bait	Tackle shop	Food/grocery	Dining	Nearby motels	Over-night slips	Ramps	Charter boats	Boat repair	Guides	Miles to Atlantic/Gulf	Credit card	Accepts personal checks
Bay Point Marina	(904) 235-6911	Gulf of Mexico	Yes	No	Yes	Yes	Yes	Yes	Yes	1	Yes	No	Yes	1/2	Yes	Yes
Captain Anderson Marina	(904) 234-3435	Gulf of Mexico	Yes	No	No	No	Yes	Yes	No	0	Yes	No	Yes	3	Yes	No
Etheridge Marina	(904) 763-6442	Masalina Bayou	No	No	No	No	No	Yes	Yes	1	No	No	No	3	Yes	No
Gulf Marina	(904) 763-3291	St. Andrews Bay	Yes	No	No	Yes	No	Yes	No	1	No	No	No	8	Yes	No
Marquardts Marina	(904) 648-8900	Gulf of Mexico	Yes	No	No	Yes	No	Yes	Yes	0	Yes	Yes	Yes	1/4	Yes	No
Tarpon Dock Marina	(904) 769-5007	St. Andrews Bay	No	No	No	No	Yes	Yes	Yes	0	Yes	Yes	Yes	2	Yes	Yes
Panama City Marina Service	(904) 785-0161	St. Andrews Bay	Yes	Yes	Yes	Yes	Yes	Yes	Yes	1	Yes	Yes	Yes	3	Yes	No
Passport Marina	(904) 234-5609	Gulf of Mexico	Yes	No	No	Yes	Yes	Yes	Yes	0	Yes	Yes	Yes	1	Yes	No
Treasure Island Mariner	(904) 234-6533	Gulf of Mexico	Yes	Yes	Yes	Yes	No	Yes	Yes	1	Yes	Yes	No	1	Yes	No
Bay Point Yacht and Country Club	(904) 234-3307	St. Andrews Bay	Yes	No	No	Yes	Yes	Yes	Yes	1	Yes	Yes	No	1/2	Yes	Yes
Rud Roys Marina	(904) 235-6911	St. Andrews Bay	Yes	Yes	Yes	Yes	Yes	Yes	Yes	1	Yes	Yes	Yes	2	Yes	Yes
Sun Harbor Lodge and Marina	(904) 785-0551	St. Andrews Bay	Yes	Yes	Yes	Yes	Yes	Yes	Yes	1	Yes	No	No	3	Yes	Yes
Tyndall Marina	(904) 283-4359	East Bay	Yes	No	Yes	Yes	No	Yes	Yes	2	No	No	No	6	Yes	Yes

Facility name	Telephone	Waterbody	Fuel	Live bait	Tackle shop	Food/ grocery	Dining	Nearby motels	Over-night slips	Ramps	Charter boats	Boat repair	Guides	Miles to Atlantic/ Gulf	Credit card	Accepts personal checks
BREVARD COUNTY																
Anchorage Eau Gallie Marina	(407) 773-1818	Indian River	Yes	No	No	Yes	No	Yes	Yes	0	No	Yes	No	10	Yes	Yes
Cape Marina	(407) 783-8410	Atlantic Ocean	Yes	No	Yes	Yes	Yes	No	Yes	0	Yes	Yes	Yes	1	Yes	Yes
Dolphins Leap Marina	(407) 783-9535	Atlantic Ocean	Yes	Yes	Yes	Yes	Yes	Yes	Yes	2	Yes	Yes	Yes	1/4	Yes	No
Diamond 99 Marina and Yacht Sales	(407) 254-1490	Indian River	Yes	No	No	Yes	Yes	Yes	Yes	1	Yes	Yes	Yes	27	Yes	Yes
Indian Cove Marina, Inc.	(407) 452-8540	Indian River	No	No	No	No	No	Yes	Yes	0	Yes	Yes	No	12	Yes	Yes
Indian Harbor Marina	(407) 773-2468	Banana River	Yes	No	Yes	Yes	Yes	No	Yes	1	Yes	Yes	No	45	Yes	Yes
Harbor Square Marina	(407) 453-2464	Barge Canal	Yes	No	No	No	No	No	No	0	Yes	Yes	No	10	No	Yes
Intercoastal Marina	(407) 725-0090	Indian River	Yes	No	No	Yes	Yes	Yes	Yes	1	Yes	Yes	No	20	Yes	Yes
Orange Cove Marina	(407) 783-8849	Banana River	No	No	No	No	No	Yes	No	0	No	No	No	1	No	Yes
Port Canaveral Marina	(407) 783-5480	Atlantic Ocean	Yes	No	No	Yes	No	Yes	Yes	1	Yes	Yes	Yes	1	Yes	Yes
South Beach Marina	(407) 723-6206	Indian River	Yes	No	No	Yes	No	Yes	Yes	1	Yes	Yes	Yes	1/2	No	No
Tingleys	(407) 452-0504	Indian River	Yes	Yes	Yes	Yes	Yes	Yes	Yes	2	No	No	No	4	Yes	Yes
Westland Marina	(407) 267-1667	Indian River	Yes	No	No	Yes	Yes	No	Yes	0	No	Yes	No	18	Yes	No
HMS Titusville Marina	(407) 269-7255	Intracoastal	Yes	No	No	Yes	Yes	Yes	Yes	5	Yes	Yes	No	20	Yes	No

BROWARD COUNTY

Facility name	Telephone	Waterbody	Fuel	Live bait	Tackle shop	Food/grocery	Dining	Nearby motels	Over-night slips	Ramps	Charter boats	Boat repair	Guides	Miles to Atlantic/Gulf	Credit card	Accepts personal checks
Jackson Marina	(305) 792-4900	S. Fork New River	Yes	No	No	No	No	Yes	Yes	1	Yes	Yes	No	10	Yes	Yes
First Performance Marina	(305) 763-8743	Intracoastal	Yes	Yes	Yes	Yes	Yes	Yes	Yes	3	No	Yes	No	0	No	Yes
Bradford Marine	(305) 791-3800	New River	No	No	No	No	No	Yes	No	0	No	Yes	No	2	No	Yes
Cable Marine	(305) 462-2822	Canal	No	No	No	No	No	Yes	No	0	No	Yes	No	1	Yes	Yes
Jackson Marine Center	(305) 584-3706	Intracoastal	Yes	No	No	No	No	Yes	Yes	0	Yes	Yes	Yes	2	Yes	Yes
Cozy Cove Marina	(305) 921-8800	Dania Cutoff Canal	No	No	No	No	Yes	Yes	No	0	No	No	No	3 1/2	No	Yes
Everglades Marina	(305) 763-3030	Intracoastal	Yes	No	No	Yes	Yes	Yes	No	1	No	Yes	No	0	Yes	Yes
Hammer Head Marina	(305) 781-7803	Canal	No	No	No	No	No	Yes	Yes	0	Yes	Yes	No	2	Yes	No
Ruffys Marina	(305) 920-0600	Intracoastal	No	No	No	Yes	Yes	Yes	Yes	32	No	Yes	No	3	Yes	No
Lauderdale Marina	(305) 523-8507	Intracoastal	Yes	Yes	Yes	Yes	Yes	Yes	Yes	2	Yes	Yes	No	2	Yes	No
Lighthouse Point Marina	(305) 941-0227	Intracoastal	Yes	Yes	Yes	Yes	Yes	No	Yes	0	No	Yes	No	1	Yes	No
Marina Bay Hotel	(305) 791-7600	New River	No	No	No	No	Yes	Yes	Yes	0	Yes	No	No	4	Yes	Yes
Best Western Marina Inn & Yacht Harbour	(305)-525-3484	Intracoastal	No	No	No	No	Yes	Yes	Yes	0	No	No	Yes	1/2	Yes	Yes

Facility name	Telephone	Waterbody	Fuel	Live bait	Tackle shop	Food/grocery	Dining	Nearby motels	Over-night slips	Ramps	Charter boats	Boat repair	Guides	Miles to Atlantic/Gulf	Credit card	Accepts personal checks
Marina 84 Inc.	(305) 581-3313	New River	Yes	No	No	Yes	Yes	Yes	Yes	0	No	Yes	No	5	Yes	No
McCulloch Boat Manufacturing	(305) 942-8074	Sea Foam Waterway	No	No	No	No	No	No	No	0	No	No	No	2	Yes	No
New River Yacht & Marina Sales	(305) 584-2500	New River	No	No	No	No	No	Yes	Yes	1	No	Yes	No	5	Yes	Yes
Pier 66 Marina and Resort	(305) 525-6666	Intracoastal	Yes	No	No	Yes	Yes	Yes	Yes	142	Yes	No	Yes	1	Yes	Yes
Pompano Beach Marine Center	(305) 946-1450	Intracoastal	No	No	No	No	No	Yes	No	0	No	Yes	No	15	Yes	Yes
Marriot Portside Marina	(305) 527-6781	Intracoastal	No	No	No	Yes	Yes	Yes	Yes	0	Yes	No	Yes	1/2	Yes	No
Riverfront Marina	(305) 527-1829	New River	Yes	Yes	Yes	Yes	Yes	Yes	No	0	No	Yes	No	2	Yes	Yes
Sands Harbor Hotel and Marina	(305) 942-9100	Intracoastal	Yes	Yes	Yes	Yes	Yes	Yes	Yes	0	Yes	No	Yes	1 1/2	Yes	No
Deerfield Island Park	(305) 428-5474	Intracoastal	No	No	No	No	No	No	No	0	No	No	No	–	No	No

CHARLOTTE COUNTY

Facility name	Telephone	Waterbody	Fuel	Live bait	Tackle shop	Food/grocery	Dining	Nearby motels	Over-night slips	Ramps	Charter boats	Boat repair	Guides	Miles to Atlantic/Gulf	Credit card	Accepts personal checks
Chucks Marina	(813) 474-4284	Intracoastal	Yes	No	No	No	No	Yes	No	1	No	Yes	No	1	Yes	Yes
Eldreds Marina	(813) 697-1431	Placida Harbour	Yes	Yes	Yes	Yes	No	No	Yes	1	No	No	No	1	No	No

Facility name	Telephone	Waterbody	Fuel	Live bait	Tackle shop	Food/grocery	Dining	Nearby motels	Over-night slips	Ramps	Charter boats	Boat repair	Guides	Miles to Atlantic/Gulf	Credit card	Accepts personal checks
Ainger Creek Marina	(813) 474-2487	Lemon Bay	Yes	No	No	Yes	Yes	Yes	Yes	1	Yes	Yes	Yes	1	Yes	Yes
Gasparilla Marina	(813) 697-2280	Placido Harbour	Yes	Yes	Yes	Yes	No	Yes	Yes	1	Yes	Yes	Yes	1	Yes	No
Sea Gull Marina	(813) 697-3000	Lemon Bay	Yes	Yes	No	No	No	Yes	Yes	0	Yes	Yes	Yes	1/2	Yes	No
Harbor Marina	(813) 625-4331	Charlotte Harbor	No	No	No	No	Yes	Yes	No	0	Yes	Yes	Yes	5	Yes	Yes
CITRUS COUNTY																
King Bay Marina and Pete's Pier	(904) 795-3302	Crystal River	Yes	Yes	Yes	Yes	No	Yes	Yes	2	Yes	Yes	Yes	7	Yes	Yes
Plantation Inn Marina	(904) 795-5797	Crystal River	No	No	Yes	Yes	Yes	Yes	No	1	No	No	Yes	10	Yes	Yes
Port Paradise Marina	(904) 795-7437	Kings Bay	No	Yes	No	Yes	Yes	Yes	Yes	1	Yes	Yes	Yes	7	Yes	Yes
Riverhaven Marina	(904) 628-5545	Homosassa River	Yes	Yes	Yes	Yes	Yes	Yes	No	1	No	Yes	No	5½	Yes	Yes
Tradewinds Marina	(904) 628-2214	Homosassa River	Yes	Yes	Yes	No	No	Yes	Yes	1	No	No	No	6½	No	Yes
Twin Rivers Marina	(904) 795-3552	Salt River	Yes	Yes	Yes	Yes	Yes	Yes	Yes	0	Yes	Yes	Yes	3	Yes	Yes
COLLIER COUNTY																
Back Bay Marina	(813) 992-2601	Back Bay	Yes	Yes	Yes	Yes	Yes	Yes	Yes	0	No	Yes	No	2	Yes	Yes

Facility name	Telephone	Waterbody	Fuel	Live bait	Tackle shop	Food/ grocery	Dining	Nearby motels	Over-night slips	Ramps	Charter boats	Boat repair	Guides	Miles to Atlantic/ Gulf	Credit card	Accepts personal checks
Boat Haven Naples Inc.	(813) 774-0339	Naples Bay	Yes	Yes	Yes	No	Yes	Yes	Yes	2	Yes	Yes	No	3	Yes	Yes
E. Turner and Sons, Inc.	(813) 262-7851	Naples Bay	Yes	No	No	No	Yes	Yes	Yes	0	Yes	Yes	Yes	2	Yes	Yes
Florida Air Boat Tours	(813) 695-4400	Lake Placid	No	No	No	No	No	No	No	0	Yes	No	Yes	7	Yes	Yes
Glades Haven Marina	(813) 695-2746	Lk.Placid Canal	No	Yes	Yes	Yes	No	Yes	Yes	1	No	No	No	3	Yes	Yes
Marco River Marina	(813) 394-2502	Gulf of Mexico	Yes	Yes	Yes	Yes	No	Yes	Yes	0	Yes	Yes	Yes	1/2	Yes	No
Pelican Bend Marina	(813) 394-3452	Johnson Bay	Yes	Yes	No	Yes	Yes	Yes	No	0	Yes	Yes	Yes	0	Yes	No
Port O Call Marina	(813) 774-0479	Gordon River	Yes	No	No	Yes	Yes	Yes	Yes	0	No	Yes	No	1/2	Yes	Yes
Port of the Islands Marina	(813) 394-3101	Gulf of Mexico	Yes	Yes	Yes	Yes	Yes	Yes	Yes	1	Yes	No	Yes	7	Yes	No
Marco River Wiggins Pass Marina	(813) 597-3549	Wiggins Pass River	Yes	Yes	Yes	Yes	No	No	Yes	0	Yes	Yes	No	1/2	Yes	No
Williams Capri Marina	(813) 394-5643	Snook Bay	Yes	Yes	Yes	No	No	Yes	Yes	0	No	Yes	No	1	Yes	Yes
Bay Marina	(813) 774-0311	Naples Bay	Yes	No	No	No	Yes	Yes	No	0	Yes	Yes	Yes	2	Yes	No

DADE COUNTY

Facility name	Telephone	Waterbody	Fuel	Live bait	Tackle shop	Food/ grocery	Dining	Nearby motels	Over-night slips	Ramps	Charter boats	Boat repair	Guides	Miles to Atlantic/ Gulf	Credit card	Accepts personal checks
Alabama Jacks Marina	(305) 248-8741	Card Sound	No	No	No	No	Yes	No	Yes	1	Yes	No	No	7	No	No
Dupont Plaza Marina	(305) 358-2541	Intracoastal	Yes	No	No	No	Yes	Yes	Yes	0	No	No	No	5	Yes	No
Florida Yacht Basin	(305) 634-0641	Miami River	Yes	No	No	No	No	Yes	Yes	0	Yes	Yes	Yes	5	Yes	Yes
Grove Key Marina	(305) 858-6527	Biscayne Bay	Yes	No	No	No	Yes	Yes	No	0	No	Yes	No	1/2	Yes	Yes
Hi Lift Marina	(305) 931-2550	Intracoastal	Yes	No	No	No	Yes	No	No	0	No	Yes	No	3 1/2	Yes	Yes
Merrill Stevens Dry Dock Co.	(305) 858-5911	Biscayne Bay	Yes	No	No	No	No	Yes	Yes	2	No	Yes	No	4	Yes	No
Miami Beach Marina	(305) 673-6000	Intracoastal	Yes	Yes	Yes	Yes	Yes	Yes	Yes	0	Yes	No	Yes	1/4	Yes	Yes
Monty Trainers Bayshore Marina	(305) 854-7997	Biscayne Bay	No	No	No	Yes	Yes	Yes	Yes	1	Yes	No	Yes	5	Yes	No
Plaza Venetia Marina	(305) 374-3900	Intracoastal	Yes	No	Yes	Yes	Yes	Yes	Yes	0	Yes	Yes	Yes	3	Yes	Yes
Glass Tech Marina	(305) 635-1509	Tamiami Canal	No	No	No	No	No	No	No	0	No	Yes	No	10	No	No
Haulover Marina	(305) 945-3934	Biscayne Bay	Yes	Yes	Yes	Yes	Yes	Yes	No	8	Yes	Yes	Yes	0	Yes	Yes
Anchor Marina	(305) 545-6348	Miami River	No	No	No	No	No	Yes	No	0	No	Yes	No	2	No	No
Atlantic Marina Boat Yard	(305) 856-4641	Miami River	No	No	No	No	Yes	Yes	Yes	0	No	Yes	No	1/4	Yes	No

Facility name	Telephone	Waterbody	Fuel	Live bait	Tackle shop	Food/ grocery	Dining	Nearby motels	Over-night slips	Ramps	Charter boats	Boat repair	Guides	Miles to Atlantic/ Gulf	Credit card	Accepts personal checks
DUVAL COUNTY																
Fisters Creek Marina	(904) 251-3306	Intracoastal	Yes	No	No	Yes	Yes	Yes	Yes	1	No	Yes	No	3	Yes	No
Chucks Boatyard	(904) 781-7133	Cedar River	No	No	No	Yes	Yes	Yes	Yes	0	No	Yes	No	1/3	No	Yes
Goodsbys Lake Marina	(904) 733-3445	St. Johns River	Yes	No	No	Yes	Yes	No	Yes	1	No	Yes	No	20	No	Yes
Jacksonville Yacht Basin	(904) 223-4511	Intracoastal	Yes	Yes	Yes	No	Yes	Yes	Yes	0	No	Yes	No	8	Yes	No
Jax Beach Marina Inc.	(904) 249-8294	Intracoastal	Yes	Yes	Yes	Yes	Yes	Yes	Yes	1	Yes	Yes	Yes	3	Yes	No
Julington Creek Marina	(904) 268-5117	Julington Creek	Yes	No	Yes	Yes	No	No	Yes	0	Yes	Yes	No	30	Yes	Yes
Lighthouse Marina	(904) 384-6995	Cedar River	No	No	No	No	No	No	No	0	Yes	Yes	Yes	20	Yes	Yes
Mandarin Marina	(904) 733-7502	St. Johns River	Yes	No	No	Yes	Yes	Yes	Yes	1	No	Yes	No	10	Yes	No
Mandarin Holiday Marina	(904) 268-1036	Julington Creek	Yes	Yes	No	Yes	Yes	No	Yes	0	No	Yes	No	30	Yes	Yes
River Boat Yard	(904) 387-5538	Ortega River	Yes	No	No	No	Yes	No	Yes	1	No	Yes	No	30	Yes	Yes
Sadler Point Marina	(904) 384-1383	Ortega River	Yes	No	No	No	Yes	No	Yes	0	No	Yes	No	30	Yes	No
Pier 68 Marina	(904) 765-9925	Trout River	Yes	No	Yes	Yes	No	No	Yes	2	Yes	Yes	Yes	14	Yes	Yes

ESCAMBIA COUNTY

Facility name	Telephone	Waterbody	Fuel	Live bait	Tackle shop	Food/ grocery	Dining	Nearby motels	Over-night slips	Ramps	Charter boats	Boat repair	Guides	Miles to Atlantic/ Gulf	Credit card	Accepts personal checks
Bells Marine Service	(904) 455 7639	Bayou Chico	No	No	No	No	No	Yes	No	0	No	Yes	No	2	No	Yes
Berkins Marine	(904) 453-2031	Bayou Chico	No	No	No	No	No	Yes	No	0	Yes	Yes	No	12	Yes	Yes
Holiday Harbor Marina	(904) 492-0555	Intracoastal	Yes	Yes	Yes	Yes	No	Yes	Yes	1	Yes	Yes	Yes	6	Yes	Yes
South Wind Marina	(904) 492-0333	Big Lagoon Bay	Yes	No	No	Yes	Yes	No	Yes	0	Yes	Yes	Yes	2	Yes	Yes

FLAGLER COUNTY

Facility name	Telephone	Waterbody	Fuel	Live bait	Tackle shop	Food/ grocery	Dining	Nearby motels	Over-night slips	Ramps	Charter boats	Boat repair	Guides	Miles to Atlantic/ Gulf	Credit card	Accepts personal checks
Flagler Beach Marina and Boat Works	(904) 439-2616	Intracoastal	No	No	No	No	Yes	Yes	Yes	0	No	No	No	25	Yes	No

HILLSBOROUGH COUNTY

Facility name	Telephone	Waterbody	Fuel	Live bait	Tackle shop	Food/ grocery	Dining	Nearby motels	Over-night slips	Ramps	Charter boats	Boat repair	Guides	Miles to Atlantic/ Gulf	Credit card	Accepts personal checks
Alafia Marina Service	(813) 677-7107	Alafia River	Yes	Yes	Yes	Yes	No	No	Yes	1	No	Yes	No	2	Yes	Yes
Imperial Yacht Basin	(813) 286-2525	Tampa Bay	Yes	No	Yes	Yes	No	No	Yes	1	No	Yes	No	15	Yes	No
River Heights Marina	(813) 251-5980	Hillsborough River	No	No	No	Yes	Yes	No	Yes	1	Yes	Yes	Yes	22	Yes	Yes

INDIAN RIVER COUNTY

Facility name	Telephone	Waterbody	Fuel	Live bait	Tackle shop	Food/ grocery	Dining	Nearby motels	Over-night slips	Ramps	Charter boats	Boat repair	Guides	Miles to Atlantic/ Gulf	Credit card	Accepts personal checks
Sebastian Inlet Marina	(407) 589-4345	Indian River	Yes	No	No	Yes	Yes	No	Yes	2	Yes	Yes	Yes	1/2	Yes	No
Indian River Marina	(407) 231-2111	Indian River	Yes	No	No	No	No	Yes	Yes	0	No	Yes	No	1	Yes	No
Sand Point Marina	(407) 664-2000	Sebastian River	Yes	Yes	Yes	Yes	No	No	Yes	1	No	No	No	1	No	Yes

LEE COUNTY

Facility name	Telephone	Waterbody	Fuel	Live bait	Tackle shop	Food/ grocery	Dining	Nearby motels	Over- night slips	Ramps	Charter boats	Boat repair	Guides	Miles to Atlantic/ Gulf	Credit card	Accepts personal checks
Back Bay Marina	(813) 992-2601	Back Bay	Yes	Yes	Yes	Yes	No	Yes	No	0	Yes	Yes	Yes	5	Yes	Yes
Boco Grande Pass Marina	(813) 964-0607	Charlotte Harbor	Yes	Yes	Yes	Yes	Yes	Yes	No	0	Yes	Yes	No	1/4	Yes	Yes
Coastal Marine Mart Inc.	(813) 694-4042	Orange River	Yes	No	No.	No	No	No	No	1	No	Yes	No	12	Yes	Yes
Compass Rose Marina	(813) 463-2400	Gulf of Mexico	Yes	No	No	No	No	Yes	Yes	0	No	Yes	No	1	Yes	Yes
Dolphin Marina	(813) 542-7097	Gulf of Mexico	No	No	No	No	Yes	Yes	No	0	No	Yes	No	10	Yes	Yes
Fish Tail Marina	(813) 463-4448	Estero Bay	Yes	Yes	Yes	Yes	Yes	Yes	Yes	0	Yes	Yes	Yes	0	Yes	Yes
Fish Trap Marina	(813) 992-6055	Fish Trap Bay	No	Yes	Yes	Yes	Yes	Yes	Yes	1	Yes	No	Yes	1/2	No	No
Four Winds Marina	(813) 283-0250	Jug Creek	Yes	Yes	Yes	Yes	No	Yes	Yes	0	Yes	Yes	No	5	Yes	No
Harbor Village Marina	(813) 997-2524	Caloosahatchee River	No	No	No	No	Yes	No	Yes	0	No	No	No	15	No	Yes
McDonald's Matlacha Marina	(813) 964-2233	Matlacha Pass	Yes	Yes	Yes	Yes	Yes	Yes	Yes	0	Yes	No	Yes	0	Yes	Yes
Jacks Marina	(813) 694-2708	Ocuchinee River	Yes	No	No	Yes	No	No	Yes	1	No	Yes	No	14	Yes	Yes
Sanibel Marina	(813) 472-2723	San Carlos Bay	Yes	Yes	Yes	Yes	Yes	Yes	Yes	1	Yes	Yes	Yes	1/4	Yes	No
Shipley's Marina & Peppertree Point	(813) 428-1349	Caloosahatchee River	Yes	Yes	Yes	No	No	Yes	Yes	0	No	Yes	No	2	Yes	Yes
South Seas Plantation	(813) 472-5111	Pine Island Sound	Yes	Yes	Yes	Yes	Yes	Yes	Yes	1	Yes	No	Yes	0	Yes	Yes

Facility name	Telephone	Waterbody	Fuel	Live bait	Tackle shop	Food/ grocery	Dining	Nearby motels	Over-night slips	Ramps	Charter boats	Boat repair	Guides	Miles to Atlantic/ Gulf	Credit card	Accepts personal checks
Tarpon Bay Marina	(813) 472-8900	Pine Island Sound	No	Yes	Yes	Yes	No	Yes	No	1	No	No	No	5	Yes	No
Timmy's Nook	(813) 472-9444	Pine Island Sound	No	Yes	Yes	Yes	Yes	Yes	Yes	1	Yes	No	Yes	1	No	No
Fort Myers Yacht Basin	(813) 334-8271	Caloosahatchee River	Yes	No	No	No	No	Yes	Yes	0	Yes	Yes	No	25	Yes	Yes
MANATEE COUNTY																
Cannons Marina	(813) 383-1311	Sarasota Bay	Yes	Yes	Yes	Yes	Yes	Yes	No	1	Yes	Yes	No	2	Yes	Yes
MARTIN COUNTY																
Bailey Boats Co.	(407) 334-0936	Indian River	No	Yes	No	Yes	Yes	Yes	Yes	0	Yes	Yes	Yes	6	Yes	Yes
David Lowes Boatyard	(407) 287-0923	Manatee Pocket	No	No	No	No	No	Yes	No	0	No	Yes	No	2	No	No
Indiantown Marina	(407) 597-2455	Okeechobee Waterway	Yes	No	No	Yes	No	Yes	Yes	0	No	Yes	No	3	Yes	No
StuartYacht Builders	(407) 283-1947	St. Lucie River	No	No	No	No	No	Yes	Yes	0	No	Yes	No	8	Yes	Yes
Whitcar Boat Works	(407) 287-2883	Willoughby Creek	No	No	No	No	No	No	No	0	No	Yes	No	3	No	Yes

MONROE COUNTY

Facility name	Telephone	Waterbody	Fuel	Live bait	Tackle shop	Food/grocery	Dining	Nearby motels	Over-night slips	Ramps	Charter boats	Boat repair	Guides	Miles to Atlantic/Gulf	Credit card	Accepts personal checks
Bud-N-Mary's Fishing Marina	(305) 664-2461	Atlantic Ocean	Yes	Yes	Yes	Yes	No	Yes	Yes	0	Yes	Yes	Yes	0	Yes	No
Curtis Marina Inc.	(305) 852-5218	Atlantic Ocean	No	No	No	No	No	No	No	0	No	Yes	No	0	Yes	No
Dolphin Marina	(305) 872-2685	Newfound Harbor	Yes	Yes	Yes	Yes	No	Yes	Yes	1	Yes	No	No	2	Yes	No
Duck Key Marina	(305) 289-0161	Atlantic Ocean	Yes	Yes	Yes	No	No	Yes	No	0	No	Yes	No	1/4	Yes	No
Garden Cove Marina	(305) 451-0649	Garden Cove	Yes	No	Yes	Yes	No	Yes	No	0	Yes	Yes	Yes	0	Yes	Yes
Holiday Isle Marina	(305) 664-2321	Atlantic Ocean	Yes	Yes	No	Yes	Yes	Yes	Yes	1	Yes	No	Yes	0	Yes	No
Key West Yacht Club Marina	(305) 296-3446	Garrison Bight	Yes	No	No	No	Yes	Yes	Yes	1	No	No	No	6	Yes	Yes
Max's Marina	(305) 664-8884	Florida Bay	Yes	No	No	No	Yes	Yes	No	0	No	Yes	No	1/2	Yes	Yes
Munro Marina	(305) 294-0088	Boca Chica Bay	Yes	Yes	Yes	Yes	Yes	Yes	Yes	0	Yes	Yes	No	1/2	Yes	Yes
Oceanside Marina	(305) 743-6666	Atlantic Ocean	No	No	No	No	No	Yes	Yes	0	No	Yes	No	1	No	Yes
Peninsula Marine Enterprises	(305) 296-8110	Atlantic Ocean	Yes	No	No	No	No	No	Yes	0	Yes	Yes	Yes	0	Yes	No
Plantation Key Marina	(305) 852-5424	Florida Bay	Yes	Yes	Yes	No	No	Yes	No	0	No	Yes	No	3	Yes	Yes
Plantation Yacht Harbor	(305) 852-2381	Florida Bay	Yes	No	No	Yes	Yes	Yes	Yes	1	Yes	Yes	Yes	10	Yes	No

Facility name	Telephone	Waterbody	Fuel	Live bait	Tackle shop	Food/grocery	Dining	Nearby motels	Over-night slips	Ramps	Charter boats	Boat repair	Guides	Miles to Atlantic/Gulf	Credit card	Accepts personal checks
HarborsideMarina	(305) 294-2780	Garrison Bight	No	No	No	No	No	Yes	Yes	0	No	No	Yes	1	Yes	No
Seafood Marina	(305) 745-1322	Gulf of Mexico	Yes	No	No	No	No	No	No	1	No	No	Yes	0	No	No
The Boat House	(305) 289-1323	Ocean & Gulf	Yes	Yes	Yes	Yes	No	Yes	Yes	0	No	Yes	No	0	Yes	No
The Marina at Hawks Cay	(305) 743-9000	Atlantic Ocean	Yes	Yes	Yes	Yes	Yes	Yes	Yes	1	Yes	No	Yes	0	Yes	No
Cobra Marina	(305) 664-4745	Snake Creek Bay	Yes	Yes	Yes	Yes	No	Yes	Yes	0	Yes	Yes	Yes	3	Yes	No
Whale Harbor Marina	(305) 664-4511	Atlantic Ocean	Yes	No	No	Yes	Yes	Yes	Yes	0	Yes	No	Yes	0	Yes	Yes
OKALOOSA COUNTY																
Hudson Marina	(904) 862-3165	Garniers Bayou	Yes	No	Yes	No	No	No	Yes	0	No	Yes	No	5	Yes	Yes
Destin Marina	(904) 837-2470	Choctawhatchee	Yes	No	Yes	Yes	Yes	Yes	Yes	1	Yes	Yes	Yes	1/2	Yes	Yes
East Pass Marina	(904) 837-6412	Gulf of Mexico	Yes	Yes	Yes	Yes	No	Yes	Yes	1	Yes	Yes	Yes	1/4	Yes	Yes
Marina at Bluewater Bay	(904) 897-2821	Choctawhatchee Bay	Yes	No	No	Yes	Yes	Yes	Yes	2	Yes	Yes	Yes	8	Yes	Yes
Marina Point	(904) 837-2090	Old Pass Lagoon	Yes	No	Yes	Yes	No	Yes	No	0	Yes	No	Yes	1	Yes	Yes
Shalimar Yacht Basin	(904) 651-0510	Choctawhatchee Bay	Yes	No	No	No	Yes	Yes	Yes	0	No	Yes	No	1	Yes	No

PALM BEACH COUNTY

Facility name	Telephone	Waterbody	Fuel	Live bait	Tackle shop	Food/grocery	Dining	Nearby motels	Overnight slips	Ramps	Charter boats	Boat repair	Guides	Miles to Atlantic/Gulf	Credit card	Accepts personal checks
Cannonsport Marina	(407) 848-7469	Lake Worth	Yes	No	Yes	Yes	No	Yes	Yes	0	No	No	No	2	Yes	No
Palm Beach Yacht Club Marina	(407) 655-1944	Intracoastal	Yes	No	Yes	No	Yes	Yes	Yes	0	Yes	No	Yes	4	Yes	No
Gundlach's Marina	(407) 582-4422	Intracoastal	Yes	No	No	No	No	Yes	Yes	0	No	Yes	No	3	Yes	No
Jib Club Marina	(407) 746-4300	Intracoastal	Yes	Yes	Yes	Yes	No	Yes	Yes	0	No	No	No	1/4	Yes	Yes
Jonathan's Landing Marina	(407) 747-8980	Intracoastal	Yes	No	Yes	Yes	No	Yes	Yes	0	No	Yes	No	2	Yes	Yes
Lotts Tackle and Marina Inc.	(407) 844-0244	Intracoastal	Yes	Yes	Yes	Yes	No	Yes	Yes	0	No	Yes	No	1 1/2	Yes	Yes
New Port Marine Center	(407) 844-2504	Intracoastal	Yes	No	Yes	Yes	No	Yes	No	0	No	No	No	1/4	Yes	Yes
Old Port Cove Marina	(407) 626-1760	Lake Worth	Yes	No	Yes	Yes	No	Yes	Yes	0	No	No	No	3	Yes	Yes
Old Slip Marina	(407) 848-4669	Lake Worth	No	No	No	No	No	Yes	Yes	0	No	Yes	No	1/8	No	No
Palm Harbor Marina	(407) 655-4757	Lake Worth	Yes	No	Yes	Yes	No	Yes	Yes	0	Yes	No	Yes	5	Yes	No
Sailfish Marina	(407) 844-1724	Intracoastal	Yes	Yes	Yes	Yes	Yes	Yes	Yes	0	Yes	No	Yes	1/4	Yes	Yes

PINELLAS COUNTY

Facility name	Telephone	Waterbody	Fuel	Live bait	Tackle shop	Food/ grocery	Dining	Nearby motels	Over- night slips	Ramps	Charter boats	Boat repair	Guides	Miles to Atlantic/ Gulf	Credit card	Accepts personal checks
Bay Pines Marina	(813) 392-4922	Boca Ciega Bay	Yes	No	No	No	No	Yes	No	0	No	No	No	1½	Yes	Yes
Clearwater Bay Marina Ways Inc.	(813) 443-3207	Intracoastal	Yes	Yes	Yes	Yes	No	No	Yes	3	No	Yes	No	2	Yes	Yes
George's Marina	(813) 784-3798	Smith Bayou	Yes	Yes	Yes	No	No	Yes	Yes	1	No	Yes	No	0	No	No
Gulfport Municipal Marina	(813) 321-6319	Boca Ciega Bay	Yes	Yes	Yes	Yes	No	No	Yes	1	Yes	No	Yes	5	Yes	Yes
Harborside Marina	(813) 360-6964	Intracoastal	No	No	No	No	No	Yes	No	0	No	Yes	No	0	No	Yes
Home Port Marina	(813) 784-1443	Gulf of Mexico	Yes	No	Yes	Yes	No	Yes	No	0	No	Yes	No	2	Yes	No
Huber Yacht Harbor	(813) 867-2117	Frenchmans Creek	Yes	No	No	No	No	Yes	No	0	No	Yes	No	3	Yes	Yes
Indian Springs Marina	(813) 595-2956	Intracoastal	No	No	No	No	No	Yes	No	0	No	Yes	No	4	No	Yes
Island Harbor	(813) 784-3014	St. Joseph Sound	No	No	No	No	No	No	No	2	No	Yes	No	¼	No	Yes
Madeira Beach Municipal Marina	(813) 393-9177	Boca Ciega Bay	Yes	Yes	Yes	Yes	No	Yes	Yes	1	Yes	Yes	Yes	2	Yes	No
Marker One Marina	(813) 733-9324	St. Joseph Sound	Yes	No	Yes	Yes	Yes	Yes	Yes	0	Yes	Yes	Yes	3	Yes	Yes
Maximo Marina	(813) 867-1102	Boca Ciega Bay	Yes	No	Yes	No	Yes	Yes	Yes	0	Yes	Yes	Yes	2	Yes	Yes
O'Neill's Marina	(813) 867-2585	Boca Ciega Bay	Yes	Yes	Yes	Yes	Yes	Yes	Yes	1	Yes	Yes	Yes	5	Yes	Yes
Port Tarpon Marina	(813) 937-2200	Gulf of Mexico	Yes	No	Yes	Yes	Yes	Yes	Yes	0	Yes	Yes	Yes	5	Yes	No
St. Petersburg Municipal Marina	(813) 893-7329	Tampa Bay	Yes	Yes	Yes	Yes	Yes	Yes	Yes	2	Yes	No	Yes	10	No	Yes

Facility name	Telephone	Waterbody	Fuel	Live bait	Tackle shop	Food/ grocery	Dining	Nearby motels	Over-night slips	Ramps	Charter boats	Boat repair	Guides	Miles to Atlantic/ Gulf	Credit card	Accepts personal checks
ST. JOHNS COUNTY																
Marineland Marina	(904) 471-0087	Intracoastal	Yes	No	No	Yes	Yes	Yes	Yes	1	No	No	No	18	Yes	No
ST. LUCIE COUNTY																
Fort Pierce Yachting Center	(407) 464-1245	Indian River	Yes	No	Yes	Yes	Yes	Yes	Yes	1	Yes	No	Yes	2	Yes	No
SARASOTA COUNTY																
Midnight Pass Marina	(813) 349-9449	Little Sarasota Bay	Yes	No	No	Yes	Yes	Yes	Yes	0	Yes	Yes	Yes	7	Yes	Yes
Venice Marine Center	(813) 485-3388	Intracoastal	Yes	No	Yes	Yes	Yes	Yes	Yes	0	Yes	Yes	Yes	4	Yes	Yes
VOLUSIA COUNTY																
Aloha Marina Inc.	(904) 255-2345	Intracoastal	Yes	No	No	Yes	No	No	Yes	0	No	Yes	No	12	Yes	Yes
Boat Club & Marina	(904) 427-3434	Indian River	Yes	Yes	Yes	Yes	Yes	Yes	Yes	0	Yes	Yes	Yes	2	Yes	No
Daytona Marina And Boat Works	(904) 252-6421	Halifax River	Yes	No	No	Yes	Yes	Yes	Yes	0	No	Yes	No	11	Yes	No
Dixie Queen Landing & Marina	(904) 255-1997	Halifax River	No	No	No	Yes	Yes	Yes	Yes	0	No	Yes	Yes	1	Yes	Yes
Lighthouse Boat Yard & Yacht Sales	(904) 767-0683	Intracoastal	Yes	No	No	Yes	No	Yes	Yes	0	No	Yes	No	2	Yes	No
Halifax Harbor Marina	(904) 253-0575	Halifax River	Yes	No	No	No	No	Yes	Yes	7	No	No	No	12	Yes	No

Facility name	Telephone	Waterbody	Fuel	Live bait	Tackle shop	Food/ grocery	Dining	Nearby motels	Over- night slips	Ramps	Charter boats	Boat repair	Guides	Miles to Atlantic/ Gulf	Credit card	Accepts personal checks
WAKULLA COUNTY																
Alligator Point Marina	(904) 349-2511	Gulf of Mexico	Yes	Yes	Yes	Yes	Yes	No	Yes	1	Yes	Yes	Yes	0	Yes	No
Marsh Harbour Marina	(904) 681-3799	Gulf of Mexico	Yes	Yes	No	No	No	Yes	Yes	0	No	Yes	No	1	Yes	No

9

PIER FISHING

Pier fishing is one of the most popular types of fishing along Florida's Atlantic and Gulf coast. All you need for pier fishing is some live bait, cut bait, jigs or spoons. Grab a rod and reel — the kind will depend on what you're after — and you're in business. If it's tarpon or sharks you're after, you'll need heavy gear. Otherwise, a good choice is a medium spinning rod with 10- or 15-pound test monofilament line.

The popping rod — a stiff baitcasting rod with a long grip — is a good fishing rig when used with a turning spool reel. Always use a wire leader when pier fishing unless you prefer a heavy monofilament leader tied to your smaller monofilament line. Many of the fish caught from piers can slice a light monofilament line with little effort: Spanish and king mackerel, barracuda, sheepshead, bluefish, to name a few.

Among the species of fish pier anglers can expect to catch are bluefish, redfish (channel bass), pompano, Spanish mackerel, king mackerel (kingfish), whiting, flounder, spadefish, weakfish (saltwater trout), cobia, sheepshead and drum. Others such as snook and tarpon may also happen by for a piece of the action.

Live shrimp is probably the most popular bait to use for pier fishing, but live fingerling mullet is excellent also — when you can buy it or catch it in your cast net. Live pinfish (sailor's choice) is good for larger fish. Another good bet is fresh mullet and the fresher it is, the better. Bluefish especially like cut mullet. Sand crabs (sand fleas) are excellent bait for whiting and other species. So are clams. Bucktail jigs and artificial grubs are good artificial lures to use for trout, blues and cobia. Small Diamond spoons are excellent for Spanish mackerel. A sheepshead favorite is a live fiddler crab.

Many of the state piers listed in this chapter rent rods and reels. Most of the piers also sell fishing tackle and bait. Most are open at night; some are open all the time. Don't overlook night fishing because often it is the best time to fish for snook and some of the others.

It's a good idea to call the pier before a fishing trip if it's a good distance away. Ask the pier operator what's being caught and when is the best tide to fish that day or night.

Bay County:

Mexico Beach Pier, P.O. Box 13425, Mexico Beach, Fla. 32410; (904) 648-5700. No rentals or bait for sale.

Brevard County:

Barge Canal Tingley's Fish Camp, 180 Fingley Drive, Merritt Island, Fla. 32952; (407) 452-0504. Rod rentals, bait for sale.

Canaveral Pier, 401 Meade Ave., Cocoa Beach, Fla. 32931; (407) 783-7549. Rod rentals, bait for sale.

Eau Gallie Fishing Pier, 1551 Highland Ave., Melbourne, Fla. 32935; (407) 254-9704. No rentals or bait.

Jetty Park Campground, 400 East Jetty Park Road, Cape Canaveral, Fla. 32920; (407) 783-7222. No rentals or bait.

Melbourne Beach Fish Pier, West End of Ocean Ave., Melbourne, Fla. 32951; (407) 724-5860. No rentals or bait.

Sebastian Beach State Recreation, 9700 South A1A, South Melbourne Beach, Fla. 32951; (407) 727-1752. Rod rentals, bait for sale.

Veterans Memorial Park, 2 E. Garden St., Titusville, Fla. 32780; (407) 267-7720. Rod rentals, bait for sale.

Broward County:

Anglin's Fish Pier, 4334 E. Tradewinds Ave., Lauderdale-by-the-Sea, Fla. 33308; (305) 491-9403. Rod rentals, bait for sale.

City of Dania Fish Pier, 100 W. Beach Blvd. Dania, Fla. 33004; (305) 921-8700, ext. 263. No rentals or bait.

Fisherman's Wharf, 222 Pompano Beach Blvd., Pompano Beach, Fla. 33062; (305) 943-1488. Rod rentals, bait for sale.

Charlotte County:

Port Charlotte Beach Pier, c/o GDC Box 2507, Port Charlotte, Fla. 33952; (813) 627-1628. Rod rentals, bait for sale.

Dade County:

Haulover Park Fish Pier, 10501 Collins Ave., Miami Beach, Fla. 33154; (305) 947-6767. Rod rentals, bait for sale.

Sunshine Pier, 1001 Ocean Drive, Miami Beach, Fla. 33138; (305) 673-7714. No rentals or bait.

Duval County:

Jacksonville Beach Pier, P.O. Box 50445, 36th Ave. South, Jacksonville Beach, Fla. 32250; (904) 246-6001. Rod rentals, bait for sale.

Escambia County:

Fort Pickens Fishing Pier, Gulf Islands National Seashore, P.O. Box 100, Gulf Breeze, Fla. 32561; (904) 934-2607. No rentals or bait.

Pensacola Bay Fish Pier, 17th Avenue, (downtown) Pensacola, Fla. 32521; (904) 432-7199. Rod rentals, bait for sale.

Pensacola Beach Fish Pier, Fort Pickens Road, Pensacola, Fla. 32561; (904) 932-0444. Rod rentals, bait for sale.

Flagler County:

Flagler Beach Pier, 215 S. A1A, Flagler Beach, Fla. 32036; (904) 439-3842. No rentals or bait.

Franklin County:

LaFayette Park Pier, P.O. Box 10, Apalachicola, Fla. 32320; (904) 653-9319. No rentals or bait.

Hillsborough County:

Ballast Point Pier, 5300 Interway, Tampa, Fla. 33611; (813) 223-8230. Rod rentals, bait for sale.

Williams Park, U.S. 41 South, Gibsonton, Fla. 33569; (813) 272-5840. No rentals or bait.

Lee County:

Bokeelia Seaport Pier, P.O. Box 517, Bokeelia, Fla. 33922; (813) 283-2011. No rentals or bait.

Fort Myers Beach Pier, P.O. Box 398, Fort Myers Beach, Fla. 33902; (813) 335-2438. (Estero Island). Bait for sale, no rentals.

Lighthouse Fish Pier, P.O. Drawer Q, Sanibel, Fla. 33957; (813) 472-4135. No rentals or bait.

Municipal Pier, 5819 Driftwood Parkway, Cape Coral, Fla. 33904; (813) 542-2185. Rod rentals, bait for sale.

Tarpon Street Pier, P.O. Box 2217, Fort Myers, Fla. 33902; (813) 334-1281, ext. 143. No rentals or bait.

Levy County:

Cedar Key Dock, P.O. Box 248, Bronson, Fla. 32621; (904) 486-4311, ext. 32. Rod rentals, bait for sale.

Manatee County:

Anna Maria City Pier, 50 Bay Blvd. and Pine St., Anna Maria, Fla. 33501; (813) 778-6030. Rod rentals, bait for sale.

Bradenton Beach Pier, Bridge Street, Bradenton Beach, Fla. 33570; (813) 778-1005. Rod rentals, bait for sale.

Rod & Reel Pier, P.O. Box 875, Anna Maria, Fla. 33501; (813) 778-1885. Rod rentals, bait for sale.

Fast Eddie's Pier, On the Bay, Anna Maria, Fla. 33501; (813) 778-2251. Rod rentals, bait for sale.

Nassau County:

Fort Clinch Fish Pier, 2601 Atlantic Ave., Fernandina Beach, Fla. 32034; (904) 261-4212. No rentals or bait.

Pinellas County:

Big Pier 60, P.O. Box 1399, Clearwater, Fla. 33517; (813) 445-0060. Rod rentals, bait for sale.

Family Pier, Fort DeSoto Park, Tierra Verda, Fla. 33715; (813) 866-9191. Bait for sale, no rentals.

Safety Harbor City Pier, 750 Main St., Safety Harbor, Fla. 33572; (813) 726-7446. No rentals or bait.

Sarasota County:

Municipal Pier (Hart's Landing), 920 John Ringling Causeway, P.O. Box 327, Sarasota, Fla. 33578; (813) 955-0011. Rod rentals, bait for sale.

Venice Municipal Fish Pier, 401 W. Venice Ave., Venice, Fla. 33595; (813) 488-1456. Bait for sale, no rentals.

Volusia County:

Ocean Pier Casino, Main & the Ocean, P.O. Box 3577, Daytona Beach, Fla. 32018; (904) 253-1212. Rod rentals, bait for sale.

Sunglow Pier, 3701 S. Atlantic Ave., Daytona Beach Shores, Fla. 32018; (904) 756-4219. Rod rentals, bait for sale.

10

FISHING TIPS

What do you get an angler for Christmas or a birthday? My mother-in-law, Nellie Farmer, gave me a large tackle box for Christmas, followed by another from my son, Kyle, for my birthday. A duplication? No way. One's my saltwater box; the other, freshwater. I have still another for surf and deep-sea fishing and a minibox with a few plugs for short trips.

Few gifts can compare with fishing tackle as far as I'm concerned. I love to open a package to find a new reel, rod, tackle box, trolling motor. My wife and sons know they can't go wrong with fishing gear for any occasion.

How can you find out what gift would be most appropriate for a friend or spouse? Ask a fishing buddy. Check with the owner or a salesman at his or her favorite tackle shop to see if any hints have been dropped. Or, more directly, while on the subject of fishing, provoke a reaction with a sly statement like, "I'll bet you have more fishing rods than one angler could ever use." You're bound to discover your fishing pal could always use something else.

If all else fails, come right out and ask.

Setting reel drag: The most important adjustment you can make on a fishing reel is to set the drag properly. Many a big fish has been lost because the drag was set either too tight or too loose.

A fishing pal, Gary Pitts, and I were trolling off Daytona Beach one day when one of the lines on an outrigger got weeds on it. I was operating the boat, so Gary picked up the rod and began reeling in the weedy balao when a fish hit another line. Gary grabbed that rod before putting the other rod down. It was a marlin, and unfortunately the drag was set too tightly and the line broke.

Use a spring scale to set the drag. Apply pressure on the spring scale with the rod held at a 45 degree angle. The drag should be set to slip when the spring scale reads 33 percent of the breaking strength of the line. For example, if you're rigged with 12-pound test line, set the drag to start slipping line when the scale registers 4 pounds.

If a spring scale is not available, there's another way to set the drag that is almost as effective. Attach the line to a fixed object and apply pressure with the line and rod. Set the drag to slip just before the line reaches the breaking point.

If in doubt, pull until the line breaks and then you will be able to set it properly the second time.

The line: While it is the least expensive part of your equipment, fishing line is one of the most important parts of your gear. Fishermen spend thousands of dollars on fancy fishing boats and hundreds more on every sure-bet lure imaginable, yet line is the key element when it comes to bringing the fish to the net.

Fishing experts at Mariner Outboards offer these tips:

Buy premium line and change the line on every reel before the season starts, even if it was used only once or twice last season. Florida anglers should change even more often because many anglers in the Sunshine State fish year-round.

Line loses strength when exposed to sunlight. Never store reels or monofilament line in direct sun. Furthermore, each time you land a big fish, cut off several feet of line and retie your knot.

Don't throw line overboard. It can get tangled up in boat props. On a sea trout trip on the Intracoastal Waterway, I had to spend half an hour untangling 30 yards of monofilament line that clogged my electric motor. Discarded line also can endanger manatees, pelicans and gulls. Burn the line in your campfire or stash it away until you can find a garbage can.

If you fish a lot, consider changing line every week, especially if you're fishing in saltwater. It takes a greater toll on the line. Tournament anglers usually change line daily. Run the line through your fingers to detect fraying. If it is frayed or even slightly worn, change it.

Don't let your line be the cause of your losing that trophy fish.

Battery maintenance: To clean your marine battery, wash down the battery case with a diluted ammonia or baking soda solution to neutralize any acid. Next, flush with fresh water, but keep the vent cap tight while doing so. The electrolyte level should be checked every 30 days. Keep the level between the top of the plates and the bottoms of the fill/vent cap opening by adding distilled water. Furthermore, wear rubber gloves and eye protection when working around batteries. Also, don't smoke around a battery that is being charged or one that has recently been charged.

Engine noise and trolling: If you're trolling offshore with an outboard engine and not catching fish, perhaps you are trolling too close to your engine. Some offshore anglers believe that you should troll some 75 to 100 yards behind an outboard because it has a higher frequency range than an inboard engine.

Calm water, fewer fish: Fish can see fishermen more clearly on calm, windless days. Therefore, when casting on a calm day, make longer casts and stay farther away from the fish you're casting to. A slight chop on the ocean makes trolling baits work more effectively when fishing offshore.

Surface structures: When fishing the bluewater of the Atlantic or the Gulf look for fish-attracting structures. The most important species that feed along the surface of the water make their appearances in the summertime: cobia, king mackerel, little tunny, dolphin and tripletail. These five are attracted to various types of artificial structures such as sargasso weed, which bunches into thin lines and even clumps, and provides shelter and shade for bluewater baitfish. It also acts as a point of reference for bigger pelagic fish.

Most saltwater structure helps orient fish in a world with no bounds and no limits. Gamefish often circle a permanent object, especially if the object attracts baitfish.

Look for anchored shrimp boats that naturally attract surface fish. These boats anchor each morning and dump unwanted small fish overboard. Shrimp boats catch about 10 pounds of juvenile fish for every pound of shrimp. That means that hundreds of small fish are fed to hungry gamefish and sharks. Fish near shrimp boats early in the morning when they are anchored and dumping their fish overboard.

Also, look for floating debris offshore. Boards, trees and cable spools will sometimes attract dozens of fish, especially dolphin and cobia. Other fish attractors include offshore buoys, wrecks and other structures that attract tripletail, cobia and dolphin. Rev up the outboard and dump a few buckets of chum overboard to attract fish to your boat.

Some innovative fishermen create their own attractors by anchoring plywood, inflatable rafts, etc. When you go back the next day you'll often find that these temporary structures have attracted schools of fish.

Offshore weed lines are formed when two currents converge and concentrate debris, trash and golden-colored weeds. The dolphin's life cycle is closely associated with weed lines. They use the weeds to hide themselves from predators. A solid weed line is always worth investigating.

To increase your chances of bringing dinner home, check out each buoy for fish on your way out and keep an eye open for floating debris.

Make shrimp look like a sand flea: When surf fish want sand fleas, here's a way to doctor your shrimp to fool even the most wily of fish. Take a fresh shrimp and pinch off the shell part of the head. Next, pinch the fan off the tail and thread the shrimp, tail first, on a No. 4 bronze hook until it covers the whole hook.

Do not detach the legs. Use a 3- or 4-ounce pyramid lead on a sinker slide. Also use a monofilament leader without a snap swivel and you have a natural-looking bait for whiting.

Sweetening the lure: When fishing for sea trout, reds and other saltwater fish that frequent the grass flats of the Atlantic Ocean and Gulf of Mexico, try this: Take a small piece of fresh shrimp and tip an artificial jig such as a Trout Tout or Mann's grub. Fish will often hit this combination when they refuse to go for a bare jig. Jigs tipped with squid are often effective for cobia.

Beware of late surge when netting a fish: Expect a last-minute getaway effort when your netted fish nears the boat. Hold your rod tip high. You may also want to loosen the drag on your reel slightly as the fish approaches the boat to keep the line from snapping.

Whatever you do, don't tighten the drag as the fish appears to tire. Take a landing net with a long handle, one that is large enough to net the biggest fish you intend to catch. Position the rim of the net so that the fish will travel directly into its center and hold the bag next to the net handle until the fish is about 2 feet away. Lead the fish into the center of the rim head first, drop the bag as the fish enters the center of the rim, move the net over the entire body of the fish and then, in one fluid motion, make one sweep upward and into the boat.

When the sun is highest, fish the deepest: Develop a pattern for fishing, especially during the hot summer months when fish move in and out of deep water. Surface lures are great for snook, sea trout, reds and other species of fish just after daybreak, during late afternoon hours and at night. However, after the sun warms the water's surface, switch to deeper running lures. When fishing with a partner, each of you should use a different lure, which you should keep changing until you come up with a winning combination.

How to dress under waders: What anglers wear under waders is as important as the waders themselves. Waders come in insulated and non-insulated versions and the wise fisherman owns both. However, you can get by with just one if you dress for the occasion. For example, anglers will stay cool in Red

Ball's Flyweight S/T nylon hippers in warm water rivers, but for cool mountain streams or early and late season outings, proper undergarments are necessary. Frigid winter waters call for neoprene waders designed specifically for that purpose.

In warm weather, lightweight slacks or shorts will suffice under most insulated waders. But in early spring or late fall, heavier pants and even long underwear will ensure comfort.

Simply put, the key is to layer clothing under your waders and be sure to keep your feet warm. Heavy socks over lightweight socks help, as do boot liners designed to retain heat and wick away perspiration. From the waist up, layered clothing also helps retain body heat. And to top it all off, it's a good idea to wear a hat to keep your head warm.

How to spook fish without even trying: Fish have a sensitive hearing system. Any unnatural noise transmitted through the water spooks them. Try to hold down the noise. One sure way to send fish scurrying is to scrape your tackle box along the bottom of the boat. Rubber strips on the bottom of the tackle box help eliminate this problem. It also helps to set it where you won't have to move it. If you have an aluminum boat, cut pieces of indoor-outdoor carpeting and cover the bottom of the boat, especially where you put your feet. Shuffling of feet, bait cans, rods, etc. can scare fish away.

Mercury Marine also has these tips: While motoring to your favorite fishing spot, cut the motor before reaching the hot spot and drift to the exact area you want to fish and then ease your anchor down into place. Or sneak up on them with your electric trolling motor.

Other practices sure to spook fish: using line that's much too heavy. Generally, the lighter the line, the better chance you have of catching fish. And when fishing shallow flats especially, don't yell at your fishing partner or to someone nearby. Loud noises are a definite no-no.

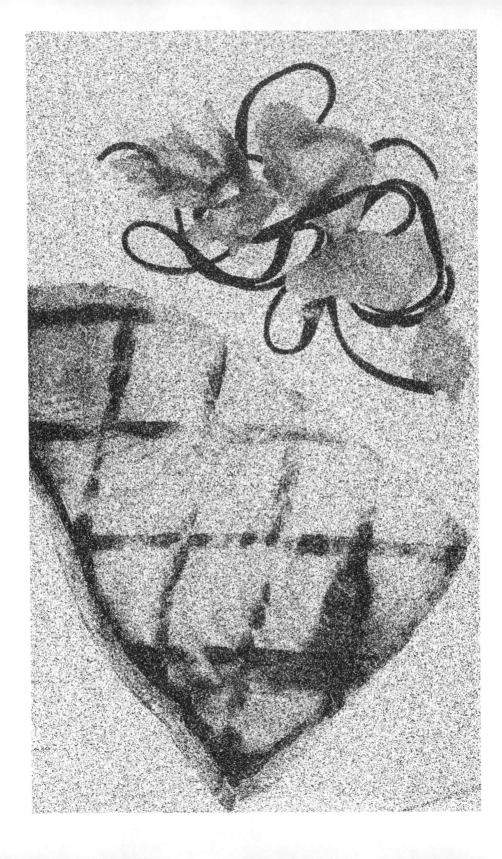

11

FISH FIXIN'S

When it comes to cooking fish, one of my favorite — and most simple — recipes is to fillet the fish, wet the fillet, dip it into some salted Alabama Corn Meal and deep fry it in some boiling peanut oil.

Toss in some Dixie Lily Hushpuppy Mix and fry some hushpuppies along with the fillets. For a real treat, serve some cheese grits, cole slaw and a big slice of Vidalia onion along with the rest of the meal.

And now for some other favorites:

FISH A LA NACHO

Grease the bottom of a pan with shortening or butter. Place several fillets on the bottom of the pan. Pour 2/3 cup of a teriyaki sauce and liquid smoke mixture over the fillets. Cover with aluminum foil and place in the refrigerator to marinate for 3 hours. When you take it from the refrigerator, add lemon pepper and chopped onion gener-

ously over the fillets. Now, pour in a can of nacho cheese soup/dip (don't add water) and sprinkle some nacho chips, bread crumbs or canned french fried onions over the top of the cheese soup spread. Bake at 375° for 20 minutes. This is a zesty seafood treat. Milder version: Use cheddar cheese soup/sauce instead.

BATTER-FRIED
SHRIMP

1½ pounds raw, peeled, deveined fresh or frozen shrimp
½ cup cooking oil
1 egg, beaten
1 cup all-purpose flour
½ cup milk
¾ tsp. seasoned salt
¼ tsp. salt
Peanut oil for frying

Thaw shrimp if frozen. Combine cooking oil and egg; beat well. Add remaining ingredients and stir until well blended. Dip each shrimp in the batter. Drop shrimp in hot deep fat (I prefer peanut oil) at 350° and fry for a half minute to a minute or until shrimp is golden brown. Remove with slotted spoon and drain on paper towel. Serve immediately. Serves 6.

CURRIED SHRIMP SALAD,
FLORIDA STYLE

1 pound cooked, peeled, deveined fresh or frozen shrimp
1 cup chopped celery
1/3 cup dairy sour cream
¼ cup mayonnaise
2 hard-boiled eggs, chopped
3 T. chopped green pepper
2 T. lemon juice
1½ T. grated onion
1½ T. curry powder
1 T. chili sauce
1 T. chopped pimiento
1 tsp. salt
¾ cup toasted sliced almonds
salad greens

Thaw shrimp if frozen and cut into halves (or thirds, if large) and combine all ingredients except almonds. Chill in refrigerator for several hours. Add almonds before serving. Serve on salad greens. Serves 6.

FLORIDA BOILED SHRIMP

2 pounds raw, headless, unpeeled fresh or frozen Florida shrimp
5 cups water
¼ cup salt

Thaw shrimp if frozen. Add water and bring to a boil. Add shrimp and reduce heat. Cover and simmer 3 to 5 minutes, depending on shrimp size. Shrimp is done when it's opaque in the center. Drain shrimp and rinse thoroughly under cold running water. Note: If shrimp has been peeled, reduce salt to 2 tablespoons and cooking time to 2 to 3 minutes, depending again on the size of the shrimp. Serve with spicy sauce.

Spicy sauce for Florida shrimp
½ cup hot barbecue sauce
¼ cup pineapple preserves

In a half-quart saucepan, combine ingredients and bring to a boil, stirring constantly. Serve hot with boiled shrimp. Makes about ¾ cup of sauce.

FLORIDA SHRIMP APOLLO

1 pound raw, peeled and deveined fresh or frozen shrimp
1 cup Italian dressing (oil base)
¼ cup honey
¼ cup maple syrup
3 T. lemon juice
2 T. soy sauce
1 T. Dijon mustard
2 T. curry powder
1 tsp. ground ginger

Thaw shrimp if frozen. Drain and pat dry. Place shrimp in shallow baking dish. Combine all remaining ingredients in a shaker jar and shake until blended. Pour over shrimp and marinate for an hour. Remove shrimp from marinade and keep the marinade for basting. Place shrimp on broiler pan and broil 5 to 6 inches from heat source for 3 minutes, basting with marinade. 4 to 6 servings.

SUPER FLORIDA SHRIMP SALAD

1 pound cooked, peeled and de-veined Florida shrimp
4 cups lettuce, broken into small pieces
2 cups diced, unpared red apples
1 cup minced celery
1/3 cup chopped pecans
¼ cup minced green onions
½ tsp. salt
⅛ tsp. pepper
4½ T. mayonnaise

1½ T. vinegar
1½ T. sugar

Thaw shrimp if frozen. Cut large shrimp in half and combine shrimp, lettuce, apples, celery, pecans, green onions, salt and pepper. In separate bowl, combine mayonnaise, vinegar and sugar; mix well. Pour over shrimp mixture and toss lightly. 4 to 6 servings.

The shrimp recipes are courtesy of the Florida Department of Natural Resources.
The following recipes are for some summer dining on the light side and are courtesy of the Gulf South Atlantic Fisheries Development Foundation.

COOL FISH SALAD

2 cups cooked, flaked fish
¾ cup mayonnaise or salad dressing
2 T. prepared mustard
2 T. lemon juice
½ tsp. sugar
⅛ tsp. cayenne pepper
⅛ tsp. dry mustard
½ cup finely chopped celery
1 apple, cored and chopped

2 hard-boiled eggs, reserve yolks and chop whites
Salad greens

In 2-quart mixing bowl, combine mayonnaise, prepared mustard, lemon juice, sugar, cayenne pepper and dry mustard. Add fish, celery, apple and egg whites and toss lightly. Serve on crisp salad greens. Garnish with egg yolks. 4 servings.

FISH 'N' MACARONI SALAD

2 cups cooked, flaked fish
2 cups cooked shell macaroni
1 cup cherry tomato halves or chopped, seeded tomatoes
1 cucumber, peeled, seeded and chopped
½ cup sliced green onions and tops
½ cup mayonnaise or salad dressing
1½ tsp. garlic salt

⅛ tsp. pepper
salad greens
lemon wedges for garnish

In a 2-quart bowl, combine first 8 ingredients and toss lightly. Cover and chill 30 minutes. Serve on crisp salad greens. Garnish with lemon wedges. 4 servings.

TASTY FISH SNACKS

1 cup cooked, flaked fish
1 cup grated sharp cheddar cheese
½ cup margarine or butter
1 T. Worcestershire sauce
1½ cups all-purpose flour
1 tsp. salt
¼ tsp. cayenne pepper
¼ tsp. paprika

In a food processor or blender, combine all ingredients and process until smooth. Using a tablespoon, form fish mixture into balls and place 4 inches apart on well-greased cookie sheet. Flatten each ball with a fork. Bake at 325° 12 to 15 minutes or until lightly brown. Makes about 25.

Some more family favorites:

SAUCY FISH KYLE

Another fish fillet specialty is a tasty combination concocted by son Kyle. It offers a zesty, succulent flavor that's hard to top.

2 pounds of fish fillets (snapper, grouper, flounder will do just fine)
1½ sliced onions
several sliced mushrooms
1 stick of butter
¼ cup of Dale's Steak Liquid Seasoning (another brand will do if that's not available)
1 or 2 cloves of garlic
¼ cup of zesty Italian dressing

Place fillets in a greased pan. Place sliced onions and several fresh sliced mushrooms on top. In a sauce pan mix and heat the butter, liquid seasoning, garlic and Italian dressing. Pour over fillets, onions and mushrooms. Broil in oven until fish is done.

TROUT A-BOB

If you enjoy a smoke taste, try this simple but tasty recipe that son Bob came up with. I often use it on sea trout fillets after an outing on the Intracoastal Waterway or the Gulf of Mexico.

Place several trout (or other fillets) on aluminum foil. Cover with a generous layer of mayonnaise. Slice an onion and place the rings on top of the mayonnaise. Sprinkle with salt and pepper to taste before folding the foil over the fillets. Poke several holes in the foil to let the smoke flavor inside. Place the foil-wrapped fish on a hot charcoal grill. Soak hickory chips in a pan of water and add wet chips to the hot charcoals while the fish is cooking to give it that hickory-smoked flavor. Close the lid and grill for 10 to 20 minutes.

SMOKED FISH SPREAD A-LA DONNA

No recipe collection would be complete without my wife Donna's smoked fish spread. Scooped up with crackers, this delicacy is a hit as an hors d'oeuvre while company is waiting for the seafood entree.

1 cup flaked smoked fish (it's especially tasty with king mackerel or mullet)
½ cup finely diced onions
½ tsp. horseradish
1 tsp. Worcestershire sauce
1 or 2 dashes hot sauce or Tabasco
½ tsp. dill weed
2 T. spicy mustard
½ tsp. lemon juice
1 cup mayonnaise
Sprinkle with salt and pepper to taste. Mix all ingredients well. Chill. Serve with crackers.

12

CONCLUSION

In this book, I have listed Florida's saltwater gamefish, where and when they can be caught in Florida's coastal waters, and what kinds of lures and natural baits they will hit best. The tips and recipes were added to make your outings more enjoyable and hopefully, more productive. It is my hope that wherever you go throughout the state this book will serve as a guide to help you find the fish that are hitting at a particular time and to help you decide what type of tackle to use. To this end, I have given coordinates of some of the state's most productive offshore reefs and wrecks. If you try them and come back empty-handed, round up a few friends and charter a boat with an experienced captain. Sharing expenses and fishing experiences can be fun and productive.

If you plan to fish the Florida Keys, Panhandle or some other area unfamiliar to you, hire a guide — at least your first time out and until you learn where to go and how to fish that particular area.

Marinas and piers along Florida's coastal waterways also have been listed to aid you in your search for a place to tie up for the night, buy fuel, tackle or bait, and to let you know where you can go to try your hand at fishing from piers or in the surf.

The chapter on fishing rules and regulations is designed to be a handy reference guide so that you don't break any of the rules during your fishing adventures. Going by the rules also helps ensure that your children and grandchildren will be able to enjoy Florida fishing as you have enjoyed it.

I wish for you as much fun as my family and I have had during the 26 years we've been fishing Florida's waters from the Panhandle to the Keys. And remember the old adage: Even a bad day of fishing is better than a good day at work!

Glossary

Aggregate limit: A total mixed catch of fish allowed under the law. For example, a combined day's legal catch of 20 striped, white and sunshine bass.

Balao: A popular baitfish, especially effective when used on trolling rigs to catch sailfish, wahoo, dolphin and other species. Also pronounced ballyhoo, the slender baitfish has a long beak or bill.

Charter boat: A boat for hire usually for offshore fishing. Individuals or private parties may charter a boat, captain, mates, tackle and bait. Most offshore trolling boats can take as many as six people.

Chumming: Chopping up bait or using whole fish or baitfish to drop overboard to attract fish.

Daily bag limit: The maximum number of fish of a particular species that you may legally catch and keep in one day of fishing. For example, the daily bag limit on snook is two during season.

Fathom: A measure equal to 6 feet.

Gaff: A device kept on board a boat to hook fish and bring them aboard as they near the boat after being hooked. It is especially helpful when fishing offshore. It has a handle — usually long — and a large steel hook attached at the end.

Grub: An artificial jig with a soft body or tail attached such as Trout Touts and Cotee Jigs.

Head boat: A boat that charges its passengers by the person, or head, for fishing. It is usually an offshore deep-sea bottom fishing boat. Many of them can facilitate 40 or 50 people and also furnish bait and rigs.

Keeper: A fish that meets the legal minimum size requirement. For example, a keeper trout.

Kingfish: The same fish as a king mackerel, but it is often referred to as a kingfish or king.

Overall size limit: A measurement of a fish from nose tip to tail tip for overall length.

Party boat: Same thing as a head boat.

Possession limit: The maximum number of fish you are allowed to have at any time. Usually the maximum is no more than a two-day catch.

Silver king: A nickname for tarpon.

Skiff: A light rowboat or a light, small sailing vessel.

Smoker king: A large king mackerel, especially good for smoking instead of frying, broiling or baking.

Stern: The aft or rear section of a boat.

Red: A term used for redfish, red drum or channel bass. It's the same fish.

Rat red: A small red. Also known as cob red. A large redfish is referred to as a bull red.

Tunny: Little tuna.

Index

A

American shad, 18

Areas, 31-32, 53-57

B

Bait

Making it look natural, 35
Pier fishing, 87

Balao, 37

Barracuda double, 38

Bay scallops, 63

Blue runner, 36

C

Clams, hardshell, 64

Closed seasons

Shellfish, 63
Snook, 60

Crab

Blue crab, 36, 63
Stone crab, 64

Crawfish, 64

D

Dolphin, 7

F

Feather and strip, 38

Fish

Amberjack, 8, 51
Barracuda, 7, 51
Bluefish, 9, 51
Bonefish, 10, 51
Cobia, 51
Dolphin, 7
Drum, 51
Flounder, 14
Grouper, 13, 51
Grunt, 51
Jack crevalle, 52

Jewfish, 52
Mackerel, cero, 52
Mackerel, king, 52
Mackerel, Spanish, 52
Ladyfish, 52
Marlin, blue, 5,6
Marlin, white, 5,6
Permit, 10, 52
Pompano, 11, 51, 52
Redfish, 11, 52
Sailfish, 4, 52
Sharks, 8
Sheepshead, 52
Snapper, 13
Snapper, mangrove, 52
Snapper, red, 52
Snapper, yellowtail, 52
Snook, 12, 59, 60
Spotted sea trout, 13, 52
Striped bass, 60
Tarpon, 10, 52
Tripletail, 52
Tuna, blackfin, 52
Tuna, bluefin, 52
Tuna, yellowfin, 52
Wahoo, 6, 52
Whiting, 52

Fiddler crab, 36

Fish finder, 39

Florida Marine Patrol, 61

G
Grouper, 13

H
Head boats, 13, 18

Herring, 37

Hooks, 14-15

K
Knots

Bimini Twist, 46
Improved Clinch, 43-44
Offshore Swivel, 44

Spider hitch, 48
Trilene, 44

L
Limits, 59-60

Line

Importance of, 43
Maintenance of, 94

Lobster, 64

M
Migration, 17

Mullet, 36

N
Netting, 96

O
Oysters, 64

P
Pier fishing, 87

Popping cork, 38

Popping rod, 87

R
Recipes

Fish a la nacho, 99
Fish 'n' macaroni, 103
Fish salad, 102
Fish snacks, 103
Fish, saucy Kyle, 104
Mullet, smoked, 105
Shrimp Apollo, 101
Shrimp, batter fried, 100
Shrimp, boiled, 101
Shrimp, salad curried, 100
Shrimp, super Florida salad, 102
Trout a-Bob, 104

Reel

Setting drag, 93

Rigs

Bottom, 38
Deep-trolling, 38
Trolling with release sinker, 39

S

Sand flea, 30, 95

Shrimp, 30, 95

Squid, 37

Strip bait, 37

T

Tackle box, 93, 96

Trolling, 35

W

Waders, 96

Where to fish

January, 17
February, 19
March, 20
April, 21
May, 22
June, 23
July, 24
August, 25
September, 26
October, 27
November, 29
December, 30

Fisherman's diary

FISH: _____

WEIGHT: _____

LENGTH: _____

WHEN: _____

WHERE: _____

BAIT USED: _____

NOTES: _____

_____

_____

_____

_____

FISH: _____

WEIGHT: _____

LENGTH: _____

WHEN: _____

WHERE: _____

BAIT USED: _____

NOTES: _____

_____

_____

_____

_____

_____

_____

_____

_____

_____

FISH: _____

WEIGHT: _____

LENGTH: _____

WHEN: _____

WHERE: _____

BAIT USED: _____

NOTES: _____

_____

_____

_____

_____

_____

_____

_____

_____

_____

FISH: _____

WEIGHT: _____

LENGTH: _____

WHEN: _____

WHERE: _____

BAIT USED: _____

NOTES: _____

_____

_____

_____

_____

_____

_____

_____

_____

_____

_____

FISH: _____

WEIGHT: _____

LENGTH: _____

WHEN: _____

WHERE: _____

BAIT USED: _____

NOTES: _____

_____

_____

_____

_____

_____

_____

_____

_____

_____

FISH: _____

WEIGHT: _____

LENGTH: _____

WHEN: _____

WHERE: _____

BAIT USED: _____

NOTES: _____

_____

_____

_____

_____

_____

_____

_____

_____

_____

FISH: _____

WEIGHT: _____

LENGTH: _____

WHEN: _____

WHERE: _____

BAIT USED: _____

NOTES: _____

_____

_____

_____

_____

_____

_____

_____

_____

_____

FISH:

WEIGHT:

LENGTH:

WHEN:

WHERE:

BAIT USED:

NOTES:

FISH: _____

WEIGHT: _____

LENGTH: _____

WHEN: _____

WHERE: _____

BAIT USED: _____

NOTES: _____

_____

_____

_____

_____

_____

_____

_____

_____

_____

FISH: _____

WEIGHT: _____

LENGTH: _____

WHEN: _____

WHERE: _____

BAIT USED: _____

NOTES: _____

_____

_____

_____

_____

_____

_____

_____

_____

_____

FISH: _____

WEIGHT: _____

LENGTH: _____

WHEN: _____

WHERE: _____

BAIT USED: _____

NOTES: _____

_____

_____

_____

_____

_____

_____

_____

_____

_____

FISH: _____

WEIGHT: _____

LENGTH: _____

WHEN: _____

WHERE: _____

BAIT USED: _____

NOTES: _____

_____

_____

_____

_____

_____

_____

_____

_____

_____

_____

FISH: _____

WEIGHT: _____

LENGTH: _____

WHEN: _____

WHERE: _____

BAIT USED: _____

NOTES: _____

_____

_____

_____

_____

_____

_____

_____

_____

_____

_____

FISH:

WEIGHT:

LENGTH:

WHEN:

WHERE:

BAIT USED:

NOTES:

FISH: _____

WEIGHT: _____

LENGTH: _____

WHEN: _____

WHERE: _____

BAIT USED: _____

NOTES: _____

_____

_____

_____

_____

_____

_____

_____

_____

_____

FISH: _____

WEIGHT: _____

LENGTH: _____

WHEN: _____

WHERE: _____

BAIT USED: _____

NOTES: _____

_____

_____

_____

_____

_____

_____

_____

_____

_____

FISH: _____

WEIGHT: _____

LENGTH: _____

WHEN: _____

WHERE: _____

BAIT USED: _____

NOTES: _____

_____

_____

_____

_____

_____

_____

_____

_____

_____

FISH: _____

WEIGHT: _____

LENGTH: _____

WHEN: _____

WHERE: _____

BAIT USED: _____

NOTES: _____

_____

_____

_____

_____

_____

_____

_____

_____

_____

FISH: _____

WEIGHT: _____

LENGTH: _____

WHEN: _____

WHERE: _____

BAIT USED: _____

NOTES: _____

_____

_____

_____

_____

_____

_____

_____

_____

FISH: _____

WEIGHT: _____

LENGTH: _____

WHEN: _____

WHERE: _____

BAIT USED: _____

NOTES: _____

_____

_____

_____

_____

_____

_____

_____

_____

_____

FISH: _____

WEIGHT: _____

LENGTH: _____

WHEN: _____

WHERE: _____

BAIT USED: _____

NOTES: _____

_____

_____

_____

_____

_____

_____

_____

_____

FISH: _____

WEIGHT: _____

LENGTH: _____

WHEN: _____

WHERE: _____

BAIT USED: _____

NOTES: _____

_____

_____

_____

_____

_____

_____

_____

_____

_____

_____

FISH: _____

WEIGHT: _____

LENGTH: _____

WHEN: _____

WHERE: _____

BAIT USED: _____

NOTES: _____

_____

_____

_____

_____

_____

_____

_____

_____

_____

FISH: _____

WEIGHT: _____

LENGTH: _____

WHEN: _____

WHERE: _____

BAIT USED: _____

NOTES: _____

_____

_____

_____

_____

_____

_____

_____

_____

_____

FISH: _____

WEIGHT: _____

LENGTH: _____

WHEN: _____

WHERE: _____

BAIT USED: _____

NOTES: _____

_____

_____

_____

_____

_____

_____

_____

_____

_____

_____

FISH: _____

WEIGHT: _____

LENGTH: _____

WHEN: _____

WHERE: _____

BAIT USED: _____

NOTES: _____

_____

_____

_____

_____

_____

_____

_____

_____

_____

FISH:

WEIGHT:

LENGTH:

WHEN:

WHERE:

BAIT USED:

NOTES:

OTHER BOOKS AND SPECIAL PUBLICATIONS OF THE ORLANDO SENTINEL

Quantity	Book	Mail price
☐	Florida Freshwater Fishing Guide By Max Branyon	$8.50
☐	Florida Home Grown: Landscaping By Tom MacCubbin	$9.50
☐	Florida Historic Homes By Laura Stewart and Susanne Hupp	$11.95
☐	The Florida Boating and Water Sports Guide By Max Branyon	$3.95
☐	The Florida Gardening Guide	$3.50
☐	Thought You'd Never Ask cookbook (Part I) By Dorothy Chapman	$10.40
☐	Thought You'd Never Ask cookbook (Part II) By Dorothy Chapman	$10.40
☐	Thought You'd Never Ask cookbooks (Parts I and II) By Dorothy Chapman	$18.95
☐	The Great Florida Adventure Catalog	$3.00

Please send me the publications as indicated above.

Mail publications to:

Name _____

Address _____

City _____

State _____ Zip Code _____

Send your check or money order to:
The Orlando Sentinel
P.O. Box 1100
Orlando, Fla. 32802